The Voice of HOPE

Heard Across the Heart of Life

by Ronna Fay Jevne, Ph.D.

San Diego, California

LuraMedia™

Also by Ronna Fay Jevne:
It All Begins with Hope:
Patients, Caregivers, and the Bereaved Speak Out

No Time for Nonsense:
Getting Well Against the Odds
(Co-authored with Alexander Levitan, M.D.)

Cover Design: Tom Jackson, Philadelphia
Cover Photograph, Text Photographs: Ronna Fay Jevne
Photograph, page 111: Courtesy of Laurie Minor, photographer for the *Guardian Express*
   with grateful thanks to Debbie and Brian Cox

LuraMedia
7060 Miramar Road, Suite 104
San Diego, California 92121

Library of Congress Cataloging-in-Publication Data
Jevne, Ronna Fay.
  The voice of hope : heard across the heart of life / by Ronna Fay Jevne.
    p. cm.
  ISBN 1-880913-09-7
  1. Hope—Anecdotes. 2. Jevne, Ronna Fay—Anecdotes. I. Title.
BF575.H56J48 1994   93-46491
152.4—dc20   CIP

Grateful acknowledgment is made for permission to reprint the following copyrighted material:

Quotation from *Theological Worlds* by W. Paul Jones. Copyright 1989. Reprinted by permission of Abington Press.

Quotation from *The Problem of Pain* by C.S. Lewis. Reprinted by permission of Fount, an imprint of HarperCollins Publishers Limited.

To Merle
A special voice
hope in our lives.
Lonna

To Norm, for pointing the way homeward

With thanks to my husband, Allen,
To whom I am deeply grateful
For he has listened and encouraged,
listened and encouraged,
listened and encouraged.
His is the voice of hope that drew me to persist with the task.

Contents

Introduction

I HAVE A PASSION TO UNDERSTAND what it means to hope. Working with the seriously and chronically ill, I have become fascinated by the resilience of the human spirit. For some, hope adds time to their lives. For others, hope adds life to their time. Yet others begin to die the day of diagnosis. Why? How is it that some people can reach deep within themselves to meet adversity while others accept the invitation to passivity or defeat?

I wanted to write the "classic" on hope. I got all the materials. Read for two years. Listened. Studied. Even got a graduate degree in theology so no one could say I had neglected to transcend my own discipline. With the mind of a scholar, I began. All the topics were there. All the big words. Paradigm. Phenomenological. Onto-logical. Epistemological. I even knew what they meant. Except as I wrote them, something was dying. The life was going out of my writing. How could the life go out of my passion? This was my life work.

Then came the interruption that changed the course of my efforts: Lynda called. She was going in for her bone marrow transplant Thursday. She just wanted to hear my voice. She was scared. She was hopeful. Risking the procedure was her only possibility for survival. She was not having an *existential* crisis. This wasn't an *ontological* issue. This was Lynda searching for hope in the uncertainty of facing death. This was Lynda reminding me of the power of hope.

In our personal worlds we each have something, to a greater or lesser degree, that helps us move forward. There are those who seem to face the future with an unending sense of positive expectations. Others are paralyzed by the challenges of life, unable to move forward. Still others seem seduced by adversity to slowly diminishing hope. It is impossible to ignore the growing numbers of people in "hopeless" situations who are not major contributors to their own destinies. Growing numbers of homeless and unemployed remind us that economic policies are not the sole solution. Mushrooming numbers of ill challenge us to face the limits of medicine. Increasing drug usage, suicide rates, and family breakdown alert us to the crisis of meaning. Starvation and environmental rape invite us to notice our unjust use of resources. Amidst the ugliness, how do we explain that individuals continue to hope?

In the heart of each of us, there is a voice of hope, a small voice that yearns to say "yes" to life. If nurtured and strengthened, it invites, encourages, pulls, pushes, cajoles, and seduces us to go forward. The experience of hope is not tidy. It is not something apart from love and courage and all the dynamics of the human spirit and human relationships. It is ever-present in our lives. Whether viewed as a human need, a biological life force, a mental perspective, or an external pull to transcend self, hope is capable of changing individual lives. It enables individuals to envision a future in which they are willing to participate.

Understanding hope is no small challenge. Hope has a unique meaning for each of us. It can't be prescribed. It can't be injected. It can't be X-rayed. It's hard to define. It's easier to tell a story about it. It *is* possible to know hope in the eyes of people, to hear it in their stories. It is as if each of us has our own Rubik's cube of hope embedded in the story of our lives – the events and people that combine with our genetic predisposition to generate a distinctive encounter with hope. By reflecting on the moments that have left an unquestionable impression on us, we can begin to see a pattern that is the personal story of how hope has been born, challenged, assaulted and enhanced throughout our lives.

As I searched to understand the pattern of hope in the lives of others, I began to trace the genesis of my passion to a period of time long before I was a professional. This book is my story of hope. The intent in sharing it is not to answer the question, "What does it mean to hope?" but rather to invite you to turn inward with me and listen to the story told by your own inner voice.

My writing is not theoretical. Rather, it is narrative. The focus is not on concepts but on sharing recollections and reflections. I attempt to profile the experiences and the people who have touched me in such a way that hope has become the window through which I observe the world. My story is not presented in perfect chronological order. Rather it is organized around clusters of experiences that speak to the development of my hope.

In the first chapter, **the voice of mother**, I introduce you to my mom, the mother of my hope. It is to the relationship with her that I owe the solid foundation of my hope. Her trust and love continue to nurture my hope.

In the chapter on **the voice of family**, you will meet the rest of my family of origin and several of my family of choice. As a rural family, we made our own play; I was at one with nature and I came to know the hope embedded in a close-knit community. It was in that community that my innocence was introduced to the reality of death.

The world of school introduced me to a world larger than that of family. It offered opportunities not only to learn academic subjects but also to observe the inequities that demoralize, that assault hope. **The voice of school** chapter also reflects how, as a teacher,

I became aware of how easy it is to become the assailant. Noticing the inequities and my own insensitivities was the beginning of my search for other ways of being.

In **the voice of intimacy** chapter, I share the birth of my awareness that I have choices in my relationships and in the meaning I create. I wrestle with aloneness in the search for connections. I confront commitment.

The voice of illness chapter includes stories of my personal introduction to the hopes of those who are marginalized. I, too, have known the quiet of impending death and the struggle to survive when the inclination to do so was absent and the outcome not guaranteed. The hope that accompanies suffering lingers all too vividly in my own life.

Those who have walked the walk are my mentors in **the voice of the "other"** chapter. They awaken me to the ways in which very small gestures can enhance hope: a reassuring word, a smile, a simple gift, a quiet *extra* moment, a hearty laugh. They also bring the disturbing awareness that equally small insensitivities assault hope. A brusque word, a broken promise, a tactlessly communicated diagnosis, an uninvited intrusion – all are weapons against hope.

The voice of the Other chapter tells of noticing the transcendent. Of the mystery that runs through my life. Of my encounters with a Presence. Of my wrestling with the glimpses of what is beyond. It is the story of my search for a spiritual home.

In exploring my journey to hope, I am acutely aware of the dichotomies of life: pain and comfort; courage and fear; caring and dispassion; life and death; faith and doubt. I am aware of moving toward acceptance of the "space between" these dichotomies as a place where the dynamics of life occur. This is the space I call hope.

I am a lover of photography. It is an experience where I find quiet. It is a lens through which I see the world. The snapshots I take are records of what holds my attention at any given time. They are glimpses into the reality that I perceive. They are the way I see the truth of my experience. Similarly, the stories I share in this book are verbal "snapshots": a series of glimpses that tell me of the world that has molded my experience of hope.

The Voice of Mother

===

THE MOTHERS OF OUR HOPE LOVE US. Their love gives birth to a world that can be trusted, a world where we can expect to have our needs met. We are fortunate if we have mothers who give voice to the messages, "You are okay; you can do things: you don't have to be afraid of life; females are not second class citizens; solutions are more important than who is to blame." They teach us with their being, not with lectures or admonitions. They are our mentors, our models. They invite us to the greater freedom of a more contemporary generation. They give birth to a self that is hopeful.

Mothers of hope love us for who we are. Our hope is stronger when we know we are loved for who we are — not loved "if" or "when" we are a certain way. When we can err and not be judged. When we know we can be different *and* accepted. When we know we can explore without fear. When we are shown the specialness of being female without having the limitations of the patriarchy in which we are living emphasized. In simple ways, like being encouraged

to love the kitchen and its smells and to know it as a place that truly nourishes.

Hope is strengthened when we are honored with a mother's pride without the obligation to be revised in order to be recognized. When we are taught without the oppression of rules. Mothers of hope can, at some point, call us friend. They can let us grow to be an equal without being a clone. They give us wings to fly without the tether of guilt. They nurture the creativity that gives our intuition a theater in our dreamworld.

I was fortunate. My mom and dad loved each other. They married in the days when women stayed at home and raised children. There was no birth control. By twenty-three years of age, she was the mother of three, two boys and a girl. I was the third. It seems like I was always confident, always moving forward. I am told I toilet trained at nine months, was a master at checkers by four, and I am still knock-kneed from my legs supporting me months too early. I seemed afraid of nothing. More than once my lack of fear was nearly my demise. I assumed that if I leapt from the table, someone would catch me. If I dove off the end of a pier, I assumed I would swim – minimally, surely I would float. Yes, there was pain. And discouragement. But my mother taught me, with her touch and her voice, that these were simply obstacles. They would pass. My mom was, indeed, a mother of hope.

She was in many ways an ordinary woman. She wrote of herself just months before her death in 1984:

> I was not born and raised on a farm. I am the classic case of the country school teacher who married the eligible neighborhood bachelor. The year was 1945. I found the adjustment from urban to rural lifestyle almost overwhelming. I missed running water, especially hot – and inside toilets. I was scared to death of pigs, cows, and even chickens. Thirty odd years later, and three children later, I am still afraid of cattle. I learned to drive a car, a truck, and a tractor. I never learned to back up to an auger. I've experienced serious farm fires, the closing of the local hall, the centralization of the community school, and the near demise of the local church. I would never have made it without my sense of humor and that of my husband's. You need a sense of humor when the cat you thought was male has a batch of new kittens on your new bedspread; when your six-year-old gives your three-year-old a hair cut; when your children have 4-H, confirmation class, ball practice, and music lessons on the same evening; when you're trying to convince your husband that you really can chase the bull by hollering through the truck window.

I joined my mother in the chaos and the stillness of her last conscious moments. She was there for me as I entered the world; I, for her, in her leaving. To be able to say good-bye with the strength of the very presence she fostered was to participate in the continuity of life. To know that life is endless, our roles short-lived. I feel the power of Einstein's words: "Is there not a certain satisfaction in the fact that natural limits are set to the life of the individual, so that at its conclusion it may appear as a work of art?"[1]

1 *Einstein: A Portrait.* Corte Madera: Pomegranate Artbooks, 1984, p. 118.

I have a lot of trouble understanding why knees have to bend to go downstairs. I know I have fallen headlong into the footscraper a dozen times, but it takes *so* long to turn around and go down backward. I don't know if I forget how or if I just want to be "growed up." It kinda hurts, but I figure if I just keep doing it, sooner or later it will work. Mom never gets mad at me, but sometimes her eyebrows go up. She just shows me over and over how to do it. I think I know how. I just haven't figured out how come my way doesn't work.

It's 1952. My dad can't sell the cattle 'cause there's some kind of disease going around. Their feet rot, I think. It's called hoof-and-mouth disease, but I have trouble saying the words. The cattle are all in a big pen just a little ways from the pump house where there's a wind mill that pumps water to the trough so they can drink. I love watching it go round and round. It seems magical. It gets muddy in the feedlot — that's what you call the place where the steers get their chop. Chop is ground up steer food. My dad grows his own.

It's kind of hard getting through the fence 'cause the boards are nailed close together. (My dad says they aren't — that I'm just chunky.) My rubber boots sink into the guk and make a funny noise every time I pull up one boot to take another step. I have a big stick in my hand. As far as I can figure, all the steers should line up to get their dinner. In a nice straight line. They aren't too hard to move even though they're big. Really big . . . 'cause Dad can't sell them until the disease in everyone's cattle is all better. I'm really little. I just go underneath and poke them in their tummies.

Mom and Carl are leaning on the fence. They both look pretty serious. Carl is quite old and he lives on the next farm. He's the choir leader, too. He looks really grumpy. I can hear my mom saying, in that real steady voice she uses when I have trouble breathing sometimes, "Come out of the cattle pen, Ronna. Put the stick down and come away from the cattle. Don't go too fast, Pumpkin. Come over to the fence."

Seems reasonable enough. It's probably time for lunch. Mom just keeps talking to me as I come closer. "Put the stick down. Let the cows have their lunch. Don't go too fast."

I think she's scared, but I'm okay. When I get to the fence, she hugs me real tight, like the time when I wandered away in that big city store. She turns to Carl and says, "How about coffee?" He is shaking his head like I did something wrong, but he smiles and picks me up and in we go.

I kind of like the ribbons. Mom always picks a color the same as my sweater. And she irons the ribbons so they look new every time. She likes me to look nice. That's not easy 'cause I'm a tomboy — whatever that means. I think it means I like horses and stuff. I like it when mom brushes my hair. She's careful not to make the tangles hurt. My braids are real long, so she turns them, kind of folds them up, and ties them behind my ears. But I don't like them that way. They look like a big question mark. I like long braids with ribbons at the end. I'm not sure why I don't tell her. Anyway, they almost always fall down after a few hours. Then I just tie the ribbons on the ends myself. Sometimes I help them *fall out* early. I think she knows.

My mom is a teacher. Well, she was before she got married. She teaches me lots of stuff. Like making brownies. She helps me measure the milk and flour and tells me when to stir. I like learning new things. Mom says she can do it faster herself, but I don't mind helpin' her. Sometimes I don't think she really wants the help, but we always have good talks. Sometimes she lets me take everything out of the baking cupboard and set up a store on the couch in the kitchen. It's an old couch with a red cover. Like the big spots on the floor. I hate the floor. But I like the red dots. The couch doesn't have a back. It's just shoved up against the wall. I get to pull it out and set up the store and stand behind it. I lay everything out — the raisins and the chocolate squares and some more raisins, yellow ones, and prunes and brown sugar. And then I sell it. There isn't really anyone to play with, so I just go around to the other side of the couch and sell the stuff to myself. The ledge on the window is where I put the money. I just use pennies from the big white glass jar with the rooster on it. It came with cookies once, but they are all gone, and now it works like a piggy bank. But just for pennies. It's easy to count them. I'm pretty good with numbers.

I like writing letters. It seems so grown up, and Mom always mails them. I just wrote my grandma a letter. My mom is reading it. I told my grandma we got a "four-stair" heating system. I don't really understand it 'cause we only have three stairs, two going down and one going up.

Mom laughs. "Sis," she says. (She always calls me Sis. I like that a lot.) "It's *forced-air*, not *four-stair*."

I frown at her. "I just spelled it wrong. Maybe I don't spell so good, but you can always tell what I mean."

'Cept this time I know I didn't really know that's what it meant. I'm not lettin' on, though.

Mom prints out the spelling for me. When I have trouble with spelling, she doesn't call me wrong. She says I spell "different." She tells me, if I want to get words right on a spelling test, how I have to spell some of them. She's a teacher, but I think she knows what it is like to be a kid. Being a kid means always not knowing something. If you can't ask your mom, it would be hard. My mom knows that, so I don't have to be scared to ask her things.

"Jacquie, I need your help in the hog barn. I've got trouble with a sow farrowing." After my dad calls Mom, he goes right back out the door. The farrowing barn is where little pigs get born. Sometimes in the winter it's too cold for them, and we put them in a big dish pan with a towel in it and bring them inside and put them inside the oven — just enough to keep them warm.

Mom glances at supper that she is getting ready. "Can you watch the liver?" she asks me.

"Sure."

"I shouldn't be long, but it if gets brown before I come back, you just take it off the burner and turn the burner off. Okay?"

"Okay." I'm proud Mom trusts me. On a farm you work as a team. That's what Mom and Dad are always saying.

"Pull the little stool over so you can see." We have a little brown stool in the kitchen so I can see things on the counter and so I can get stuff from the cupboards by myself. It's wooden and it was never painted, so it looks pretty old. I'm sort of short for five. Well, four-and-a-half or so. I'm not sure how long it is until my birthday, but it's cold outside so it can't be too long.

I'm watching that liver really close. I wait and wait for it to be brown on top. It's still not brown when Mom comes back. I am still watching that pan. I haven't taken my eyes off it. Mom takes the egg turner and turns the liver over. It's burned. Burned bad. She says, "Oh, Sis, I'm sorry. I meant brown on the *bottom*." Something sinks inside me, and it aches from just above my belt right up to my shoulders. Kind of like when something really sad happens. I feel bad.

"Sis, it's not your fault. Sometimes mommies don't give very good instructions, do they? Mom forgot to tell you brown on the underside."

She lifts me off the stool and plunks me up on the counter beside the stove. "Now what else do you figure we could fix for supper?"

I am in my bed upstairs. I have a room by myself. It's in the old log part of the house. They put plasterboard over the logs, and it has pretty wallpaper on it. Ballerinas. Mom and I picked it out. She said they would keep me company at night and that I could make up stories about them. But there are spaces between the logs and what's over them. That's where the mice play. I never open the little closet behind my blue bedside table. Mom said not to cause of the bats. I hate bats. It's like the bats and mice are all part of a little village that lives behind my walls. At night I pretend that the bats are giving a concert for the mice. That's how I explain the squeaks and the pitter-patter, or whatever you call the sound of mice running back and forth. Sometimes I have nightmares. When I wake up, that's the first thing I hear. When I try to scream, nothing comes out. My chest just pounds. I want someone to hear me. But I am screaming only inside. Only the darkness hears me scream. I sit up. I'm too afraid to go across the squeaky floor boards, down the stairs. I have to go through the dark kitchen, and the floor is cold. That's the only way to get to Mom and Dad's room. If I get that far without a monster getting me, they will let me into their bed. And I'll be safe. But it's so far. I bite my lip and squinch my eyes closed. Mom told me when it happens, if I concentrate real hard, I can play Walt Disney cartoons in my head and get the ballerinas to dance with Goofy and Mickey Mouse. That way I will go back to sleep pretty soon. It's hard though, 'cause it's so dark. But it works. Mom was right.

I like it when Mom comes up to my room and helps me figure out what to wear. She sits on the bed sometimes, and I hold up things and ask, "Does this go with this?" I can't figure it out easy for myself, but I am learning. Today she says, "Why don't you put all the things of the same color in one pile." I already know to put my pants in one drawer and my blouses and sweaters in the other and my socks and shorts in the little drawer and to keep things that are the same together. It helps a lot when I am trying to figure out what to wear. Mom has been getting me to put out what I am going to wear the night before, too. She says it's real important for kids that are hyperactive like me. It helps, too, 'cause there isn't any heating right into my room, so in the morning I can just grab my stuff and get dressed over the big heat register in the living room. And I know not to wear plaids with stripes. I don't wear stripes that go around me either 'cause that makes me look "chunky."

I am getting to be a pretty good cook, too. I entered four things in the fair: a school lunch, date squares, some salad dressing, and something else that I forget. I guess I forget the one I didn't win a prize for. The school lunch had a wiener in hot soup in a thermos so that when you're are ready for lunch, your hot dog is hot. Mom saw it in a book and showed it to me. She said it was all right to borrow ideas from books. I won first prize for the best school lunch.

I am at my piano recital tonight. I know my piece really well, but it's a little hard to play 'cause I sprained my finger pretty badly playing ball yesterday. I didn't mean to. I just caught a hard drive when I was playing short stop. That's my favorite position.

I'm wearing my new dress with lace on it that Mom made me. My hair is in really nice kind of ringlets. Mom did it. She had to fix it 'cause my hair got wet in a hail storm this afternoon when I was at a birthday party.

It was Lily's birthday. It was a really hot day, but the sky was clouding over. It looked like a storm was coming but not for a while. It was pretty dark in the west. That didn't stop us from playing ball. I love playing ball. Only I had a problem. I was running as hard as I could for home base. I was sliding really well. I knew I was beating the ball to the catcher. I felt the base move under the soles of my feet. Ah ha! I made it. My head turned to see by how much. To see where the ball was. For a moment, I couldn't feel anything. I just lay there, my hands clasped over my right eye and cheek. I don't think I even moaned. In a way it didn't hurt. It just felt numb. Lily's mom seemed to come from nowhere. Just then it started raining buckets, and before we got inside it was pounding hail. We were soaked. The kitchen was old, but I didn't look at it much. I had to hold a bag of frozen peas on one side of my face. It still didn't hurt too much.

When my mom came for me, she just looked at me, smiled, and shook her head. She didn't frown or ask me a whole bunch of questions. She just said, "I don't think your face will go too well with the color of your new dress." We took another bag of frozen peas with us. But it still got all black-and-blue really quick.

I suppose that's why the audience is laughing as I curtsy at the end of my piece.

The University Hospital is forty miles away. We come here every Thursday morning. We are waiting my turn. They are trying to fix the scar on my cheek. This one came from goofing around on the ice. The skating rink is just outside the gymnasium door, in the corner of the school grounds. I'm a good skater. I can stop and start really fast 'cause I have figure skates. Richard was just trying to get his ski hat back when we fell. Cutting my face wasn't really his fault. We were playing "keep away" with his hat. I didn't really even feel the cut. That whole side of my face just went numb. I wasn't scared. Well, a bit. There was a lot of blood. I took off my mitten and put two fingers right through the hole in my cheek. Then I was a little more scared. Even when the doctor stapled it shut with two big clamps, it still didn't hurt. It hurt more getting the staples out. The scar is pretty big and it's real red. Mom calls it my "character mark." She makes it sound like everyone has a character mark. But I know they don't. She has a way of making everything seem like it's going to be okay.

I lean against the counter while Mom is getting afternoon coffee. In a Norwegian home you never miss coffee. That means sandwiches and cake and cookies and maybe even fruit. I do most of the baking on the weekends. That's my job in the house. She listens to me tell her about Trudy.

"Trudy's from one of the schools out west that just closed this year. You know, one of the one-room schools like we first went to. None of those kids can spell or write as well. But the teacher is awful to her. When she asks Trudy to read out loud, Miss T. just stands there and smirks. She says little things that make Trudy look stupid. Mom, she's not stupid. She's just shy, and she doesn't read so well. When Trudy said she would run for student council secretary, Miss T. said right out in class, 'You shouldn't be allowed to run. You aren't bright enough and you can't spell. This is just silly.' Trudy was really embarrassed. Mom, that's wrong. Miss T. shouldn't be allowed to do that. Trudy should be able to run if she wants to. Right?"

"Right."

"Well, can Miss T. keep her from running?"

"No."

"Well, I wish she'd run."

"What are you prepared to do about it?"

I never thought about what I could do. I thought Mom or maybe Trudy would do something.

In my silence Mom added, "Think about it."

"Okay, I will."

Two weeks later, it feels good to stand in front of student council, gavel in hand. Trudy is beside me. I am president. She is secretary. I bring the meeting to order.

I come home almost every weekend. It's my first year of college. In some ways I am a competent young woman. I'm only seventeen, but I have a little red Volkswagen that Mom and I each paid two hundred dollars for. Since it gets pretty cold in the winter, Dad put two batteries in it, and it has a gas heater.

It's nearly seven when I arrive home. It's already dark. They have waited supper. The boys and Dad are sitting at the table, just talking. The smell of supper is coming from the oven. I've just taken off my coat, and Mom asks, "Sis, will you take the casserole out of the oven? The salad is on the table."

"Sure."

Oven mitt in hand, with my usual deftness, I whip open the oven door and pull the rack forward, totally oblivious to the laws of physics. The casserole plummets to the floor. The best I can do is hope for an upright landing. No such luck! I have that look on my face that says, "I know. My body is way ahead of my brain — again." It's not that I deliberately cause accidents. It's just that they seem to happen a lot. Somehow I thought going to college would make me less accident prone. It doesn't seem to have changed anything. Mom simply smiles. She doesn't even raise her eyebrows.

"Glad you're home, Sis. We've missed you." She turns to my brothers and Dad who are recovering with laughter and asks, "How do you feel about beans?"

At nineteen I am already married. We are home for a weekend visit. As always, Mom and I are partners in the kitchen. Then comes the predictable, "Run downstairs and get the potatoes."

I feel ten years old again! I muster up the courage to say, "I hate running downstairs and getting the potatoes. I have been doing that as long as I can remember. I'm the 'run over' girl. Run over and get this. Run over and get that. I'll go, but I hate that job. Do you know what it was like for me as a little kid to go down there? Often as not it was dark, the spuds were spoiling. The fresh sprouts were like tentacles that wrapped around my wrist when I finally found a good potato and pulled back quickly. I hated picking up a potato that broke like a ripe boil in my hand. It felt awful, especially in the dark. That place used to scare the blazes out of me as a kid."

"Sis, you never said."

"I didn't want to be a sissy."

Off she goes for the potatoes. Our relationship is forever changed. Later that day she makes a proposal. It's simple: "You grow up and I will let you."

It's working very well.

At twenty-six I have been divorced for three years. I'm not sure how my folks will take to me uprooting myself to go to Arkansas for a new relationship. They have never met Ron. Their response won't be a deciding factor, but their acceptance would make things easier. Might as well open the letter. I deliberately make a cup of hot tea. I have only a couch and a chair. I go to the green plaid chair. I put my feet up on the ottoman. The letter is in a standard envelope. I wish I had a letter opener. It seems like special letters should be opened with a letter opener. I tear back the end and slip out the letter. It's on Mom's special note paper:

Dear Sis,

This is not a good time for me to try to write a letter, as it is Monday night after a harried weekend of housecleaning, company, Christmas planning. I'm tired and realizing that, for the first time, I'm not looking forward to going to work tomorrow.

However, I do want to acknowledge your letter and tell you that I do share your joy and wish you the best in this new adventure. It sounds like a sensible approach (to the exploration of a new relationship). Of course, I have some protective feelings – like I wish you were a four-year-old asleep upstairs, and I could tuck you in and know you were safe – but you are not only 26 years old, you are a mature woman making her own decisions. And your batting average is pretty good. Of course, I wish you were going to be closer, but that would be selfish. (I keep wondering who I am going to talk to.) And I wish I knew Ron better, but it's much more important for you to know him well.

Fly, darling – it beats the blazes out of pecking around on the beach. I'll miss you – God, how I will miss you.

Love – so much love,

Your mother

She was always hesitant about the heart surgery, yet the fatigue was getting debilitating. There is apparently no real option. The call has come. The bed is booked. Mom has finished all the Christmas shopping. We have been to the farm two nights before for one of her simple but special meals: homemade chili, a fresh salad, homemade pie. Val, her best and lifetime friend, joined us. They have been together through many a difficult time.

On the way out the door, she taught Dad to use the dishwasher. On the way into the city, she stopped at the Butterfly Shop, her favorite clothing store in the little village near the farm. A blue nightie and new dressing gown. In the few hours before going to the hospital, we shopped at the mall for yet another gown. So gently, she smiled when I encouraged her to buy the bed jacket.

"You are just trying to make your old mom feel better." My *old* mom was only fifty-eight. We walk the halls until visiting hours are over. I hug her as I have never hugged her before. She looks me square in the eye and says, "I am not going to cry."

Surgery is tomorrow. Everything should be fine. The survival rate is over ninety-five percent, and she has no known additional risk factors. I have such a restless night. I awake from a dream:

A carriage pulled by six teams of white horses has come for Mom. This is no ordinary team: Their bridles are polished, and they step in near-perfect unison. This is no ordinary coach: There is brass on the corners, and there seems to be no driver, just a coachman on the side. Surely they have come for royalty. As I am waiting for Mom to come out from the estate house, the carriage is transforming. It is taking on qualities of a hearse.

I awaken, a sense of dread weighing heavily in my chest. A dream of several weeks ago returns to my awareness. In the midst of a South Pacific tidal wave, I had heard the words, "I need a stillpoint," and found myself in a misty and mysterious veil of safety. The messages from my unconscious seem contradictory. What will the day bring? I conclude: Mom has taught me to worry only about those things that are within my control. She has taught me to live without fear. I need to be hopeful.

The phone rings all afternoon. We are either making calls or receiving them. The day is like a blur and yet incredibly vivid. The cautious tone of the nurse who answered my morning inquiries. The dream-like reality of being at my mom's shoulder while the code team worked like synchronized automatons whose tasks demanded they transcend any feelings about the repulsiveness of the lifesaving efforts that were transpiring. The sense of everything happening in a moment of time that had stopped. The eternity of the moments of racing down the corridor alongside her stretcher, holding some piece of equipment the function of which I can't recall. Meeting the eyes of the young physician as the doors to the surgical unit opened. Mom and I parted there. I looked earnestly at him. "Take care of my mom." His eyes met mine and I saw his despair. The aloneness of the walk back to the waiting room. The aloneness. Then the phone call to Dad.

It's only hours later, now. It feels like decades later. The doorbell rings. I open the door, and there stands my friend Cheryl. She steps in and hugs me. There's a stronger bond in her hug than we have ever spoken. Her words are words I need to hear: "Thank God there were women like your mom, so there could be women like us." Somehow she knows that "I'm so sorry" are not the words that will comfort. She knows to call on strength. I feel the strength of the tribute. Yes. The task of healing will be to celebrate my mom's life. Still, her death leaves me seemingly alone.

A whole era of my life is coming to an end. There will be no more smell of cinnamon buns in the kitchen when I go home to visit. There will be no more homeknit sweaters. There will be no more special winks to say, "You look great," or "I am proud of you." There won't be those precious occasional hours to shop together. For my brothers, there will be different spaces to fill. Dad will do his best, and it will be an admirable effort, but I only get one Mom. It will be no less painful for my dad.

As I stand at the podium to deliver her eulogy, I am still not sure if I can compose myself for the task. I wonder, "Who are all these people?" Six hundred people await my words. I can't speak. It's not tears. It's the sense of not being able to swallow. The first words I say are, "Bear with me should my voice break." Then I feel her strength and poise. I am once again in "the stillpoint." I speak calmly and conclude with these words:

> Each of us has our own memories of my mom. As a child, my memories are of her tolerance to teach me; her intolerance for untidiness and bad manners. As I grew older, I remember her encouragement to question and experience, her discouragement of prejudice; her rare creativity and ability to make events so special, with such apparent ease. Truly, this was a remarkable woman. Perhaps most remarkable was her ability to clearly let each of us know that we counted; she touched our lives in a way that made us different, forever. She always had enough love to go around. It was never hard to share her. She didn't talk much about her philosophy. She simply lived it.

The Voice of Family

FAMILY IS WHERE WE FIRST MEET THE "OTHER," where we first experience who we are in relation to those on whom we are not totally dependent. Family is where we have a place but not the sole place. It is where we learn it is a two-way street, that the world is not solely our territory. In a family there are boundaries as to what we can do, where we can be. It is where we learn our roles and our place. Where we are affirmed by participating in the daily tasks of life and where we share in joy and in humor — and in tragedy. It is where we can safely test our limits, where risk and hopes are linked, where playfulness finds its first playmates.

Families of hope allow us to experiment with our creativity and to err in our judgment. Families of hope confirm that we are lovable. They send the message, "You belong; you have a place here, a valued place. You are part of something larger, perhaps even something greater." From them, and with them, we learn that the world is a place where we can experiment and share. They give birth to a self that is confident and risking and connected.

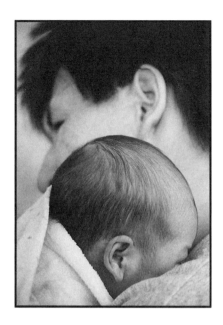

Families of hope can extend beyond our parents and siblings. Someone down the road or down the block may be extended family. Special people become "family of choice." They, too, care for us. Value us. Protect us and laugh with us and guide us. If they are numerous, we may experience being "a child within community." We come to understand that hope happens in community. In a community of hope, there are options. Places and people to connect with as we move to being part of the larger society. If we are fortunate, our family of hope extends beyond human relationships, and we experience being "a child of the universe." We feel a bond with the earth, with all that is living. With the mystery.

It is in our families that we first meet the dichotomies of life, that we first begin to know the "spaces between" where the dynamic of hope is played out: belonging and separation, connection and silence, risk and security, me and other, past and future, life and death. We learn that what we have loved we can also lose. That no one in the family is immune. And no one has control over death. When death reaches into family, we learn that the comfort of belonging and the joy of loving are coupled with the pain of separating. When death reaches into family, life has new meaning.

The inner circle of my family of hope is where I learned to laugh and learned to risk. Where I came to know that playfulness and humor are part of the day. Where I accepted the same risks and challenges as my brothers. Where I was my brothers' equal — yet not always. Where I learned the specialness and the separateness of being female. Where I learned that being a girl is different from being a boy, somehow more and somehow less, but undoubtedly constrained. Where I learned that there is a place for me with my dad. A place different from my brothers', but a special place. Where I learned that men, too, feel.

I felt safe not only with my immediate family but with the world that became my family. I learned that the boundaries of family can be widened. That other people can be included. Like Claude. And down the road lived Aunt Milly and Freeman and a community that cared. That my family of hope can include all that I relate to. My dog, my favorite tree, the universe itself.

As a farm child, I came to know the natural cycle of life: Things are sown and reaped. Animals are birthed and marketed. Seasons come and go. The wonder and solitude of nature became my friend. Nothing needed to make sense. I asked a trillion questions, but the answers didn't much matter. I had my own ideas about why the moon changed shape and why leaves turned colors. I just inhaled life.

I began to see and sense the pain of loss, feel the puzzlement, have the questions, experience the estrangement. I learned the power of silence so accidental in the midst of grief. The big griefs joined the smaller griefs. I already knew love. The hope was for inclusion; for understanding. For a sense that, "Yes, I belong. Yes, I fit." The hope was a longing, a deep puzzling longing.

I ride on the John Deere tractor with Dad sometimes. It's an old green tractor. Dad has to help me get up 'cause the step is so high. I sit on the tool box. It's old. There's no paint on it. It's not greasy, but it's like there is a lot of oil in the wood. That's where my dad's tools are. And I sit on the top. It's just the right size. I can sit with my elbows on my knees and my chin in my hands and yell at my dad. I don't know if he made it just so it would be the right size for me, but maybe. The tractor sure is noisy. Sometimes it kind of puts me to sleep 'cause Dad can't hear my questions. When he does, he shouts back the answers.

In the afternoon we stop and have lunch in the field. Mom always puts in some Kool-Aid 'cause I don't drink coffee. I don't know any little kids who do. I can eat just as big a lunch as my dad does. There is always a cookie or something left over for Tip. He's our dog. He's as big as me. After lunch we climb back up on the John Deere and work till supper. When I get home, I am really grubby. That's what happens when you work in the field all day. You get real grubby. But my dad needs the help.

I love going to the stockyard. Every Tuesday Dad takes one of us. He buys pigs from the other farmers and puts the pigs on the train at the end of the day. The pig pens are like a puzzle. The gates open all different ways so you can get the pigs to go anywhere you want. Sometimes you have to yell at them. I love the pig scales. They are way taller than me, and they look like something I saw on TV. When Dad moves something back and forth on a scale's big arms, everyone is kind of quiet, and when he finishes, the farmer almost always nods his head. If I get tired, Dad takes me up to my grandma's. She says we smell when we come from there, but she likes us to come anyway. Dad comes later. He always brings my grandpa and grandma some money and some cream from our farm.

One Tuesday night we had trouble with the truck on the big hill. The hill's big 'cause there is a dam to keep water in just a little ways away. Dad calls it the "dam" hill. We didn't get home until six in the morning, and I marched in and said to my mom, "I want my supper!" I had never stayed out all night before. I wasn't scared or anything 'cause my dad was there.

It all started when Dad dumped a whole pile of gravel down by the hog barns. I like the feel of gravel, and I like the big yellow toy dump truck best. You can push it where you want it to go, and all of the wheels turn. We started building a whole set of roads for a trucking company that we are going to run! Tom — he's my oldest brother — is the head of the company, and my brother Nels seem to know where the roads are supposed to go. I'm the cook on the crew. The gravel doesn't make good mud pies, though. I have to go and get real dirt and mix it in. I know its my job, but I like building roads better.

Then I get sick. I can't even go out for a couple of days. I hate being sick. I'm so bored. There aren't any animals to pet. And TV doesn't even come on until five o'clock. Howdy Doody is kind of dumb, anyway. I like Roy Rogers, but he's only on on Fridays. Boy, I wish I had a horse like Trigger.

Finally, I am back outside. Tom and Nels take me down to the trucking company.

"Wait till you see what we did." In a minute, I see. All my roads have black stuff on them. "We paved them all for you."

"Oh," I say hesitantly, "thanks."

"We got all the old coal and carried it over and smashed it and paved all your roads first."

It is hard looking happy. *I want to pave my own roads!*

I love going to Co-op stores with my dad. He has to go and talk with managers and stuff, and then he goes to a meeting in Saskatoon every month. That's a long ways away. He goes even if it's harvest. When we walk into the stores, all the clerks straighten their uniforms. They aren't really afraid of him. Just sort of extra nice. This time, when he's finished, we're going to the King Edward Hotel for lunch.

The waiter has a black suit on. Like my dad wears when somebody dies. Except the waiter has a funny tie.

"For two, sir?"

"Yes."

There is a carpet on the part of the floor that we walk on to get to the table. Where we are eating is kind of dark. I like sitting in a little booth. My feet can't touch the floor, not even my tippytoes. There are two tall glasses in front of my plate that look a lot like what Mom and Dad drink wine out of. The waiter puts water in one of them and takes the other one away. I can't read, but I know Dad is ordering something grown-up for both of us. All the food comes on little silver trays. Potatoes with little green stuff on one and broccoli on another. It looks pretty, but I sure wouldn't want to do the dishes. And there is more than one fork and more than one spoon, and the bun is on a plate all by itself with a knife just for your bread.

When we finish, Dad asks, "How did you like that, Princess?" He usually calls me "Newkins," but I know he doesn't really think I am a nuisance.

Whenever we go to Calgary to visit my grandparents, we have Cokes and ham sandwiches in the car. Usually we aren't very far from home when we're laughing and already starting to eat our lunch. It's kind of fun. It's like a moving picnic. Mom always uses fresh white bread and puts lettuce in. And she uses store-bought ham. So it's all kind of special. Tom and Nels and Dad play a game where they guess the kind of car that is coming down the highway. They are pretty good at it. We talk all the way to Calgary. Lots about the farms and animals. Tom is going to be a farmer when he grows up. A dairy farmer with lots of cows. Like the Krauses. Dad asks me, "What are you going to be when you grow up, Newkins?"

"I don't know yet, but I am going to be in a history book. I just don't know what for yet."

I can see his eyes in the rear view mirror. He doesn't believe me. I thought my dad believed I could do anything. Are there things I can't do?

When I get mad at my mom, I 'hack my little orange hootcase' and move over to Milly's. Sometimes I go just 'cause it feels good. It's a whole mile away, and it takes a long time to walk there. I think Mom calls Milly to tell her I'm coming. Tip goes with me. He understands that ditches are wonderful places. I like to watch a leaf flow through a culvert, and I can see just how far to go before the water goes over my rubber boots. I like the sound of the stubble when I walk through the field, too. And I can stop and see if the corn is higher than I am.

Milly doesn't have any girls, just four boys, so my visits are special. Sometimes I even stay overnight, and she makes gingerbread men. I save them for a long time. After a while their heads break off, so I have to eat them.

Mom sometimes comes, and Mom and Milly and me do things together. Like clean chickens. My hand is just the right size for digging out the lungs! You just take your finger beside your thumb and push down and it slides right under the chicken's lung. The lung is kind of mushy when it comes out. We make lefse, too. That's flat bread made from potatoes that you put through a masher that makes the potatoes go all squiggly. When we have a lefse-making bee, Milly even lets me carry the lefse on the lefse stick right across her big kitchen. And that's hard 'cause it could fall off the lefse stick and you'd have to start all over. I never drop it. Not once.

My brothers and I invent lots of our own games. We like trying new things. Sometimes we don't think them out too well, though. They seem exciting, but they aren't so smart. Like the dart game we thought up. Our clothes shoot is an old dumb waiter. You just open the little door in the back porch, and your dirty clothes drop to the basement. There is a door at the bottom. It isn't on hinges. You just sort of lift it out. You put your fingers in the holes that are there for lettin' the air get in and then pull the door out. The dart board hangs just above it. The whole place is kind of grungy. The sump pump is down there, and that's where the men take off their smelly clothes, but we still play there sometimes when we can't go outside. We have only four darts so we have made up another part to the game. One person gets behind the door in the clothes shoot and watches the other person, through the air holes, throw the dart. Just when the dart is being is thrown, you push out the door, pop up, and dodge the dart. Well, it's pretty exciting. Tom winds up, chucks the dart. It isn't all that hard a throw. Nels pops up. Wrong timing! He doesn't get out of the way. The dart sticks in right beside his eye. Just in the corner beside his nose. We just look at each other, the dart dangling on Nels' face. No question. We all agree. This calls for a mom. We traipse upstairs. Tom first 'cause he's the oldest.

Mom is standing at the sink. Tom says, "Mom," kind of slow and lets his voice go up at the end. She turns. Nels smirks past the dart.

"What have you been doing now?"

"Nels kind of got in the way of a dart."

Mom shakes her head. She points to the kitchen chair and says, "Sit down. And don't touch." She disappears into the bathroom. None of us say anything. She comes back with a bottle of that red stuff you put on cuts. When she takes the dart out, it doesn't even hurt Nels. Then she asks, "How did this happen?"

Tommy tells her, and we have to promise not to play that game again. It really helps that she doesn't get mad.

Animals can talk, you know. Just watch their eyes. Especially dogs. When they bark, they aren't really talking. They talk mostly with their eyes. Tip is my dog. Well, I guess he is everybody's dog. But he is sometimes mine for a while. Tip's big. He's a collie. Sort of. He's bigger than a collie. His nose isn't so pointed, and his fur is thicker. During the summer, we cut his hair with the sheep sheers so he won't be so warm. It doesn't look so good the first time. I don't think he's ever had a hair cut before. He stands really, really still — like he knows it is important.

Tip likes walking with me. We go down the lane a lot, even though Mom likes it better when I go into the field. I always take an extra sandwich for Tip. He likes me to share. He sits on the side of the ditch with me and eats it real proper. In little pieces, 'cause that's the way I give it to him. He likes peanut butter. I don't so much. It sticks to the top of my mouth a lot, and it's hard breathing if you take too big a bite. I talk out loud, and Tip talks with his eyes. It's easier for him 'cause I'm taller. It works that way. 'Cause I can see his eyes and he can hear really good. He's kind of lonely, too, 'cause we don't have another dog. Sometimes I wonder if he would like another dog to play with. I wish I had someone else to play with at times.

Dad bought Lady 'cause she is specially trained for kids. You can slide off over her tail, crawl under her legs, hang onto her mane, and she doesn't flinch. She's a bit finicky, though. She only lets kids catch her. That sort of bugs Dad when he wants to use her for cutting cattle early in the morning. I like it when he comes up to my room real early and gets me up to catch her. I like those times, just Lady and Dad and me. When you walk on the grass, it kind of crunches. Sometimes I get up early and go riding all by myself. I'm just ten, but I go down to the lake banks. It's really beautiful when the sun comes up. It's like you don't only *see* it come up, you kind of *hear* the world waking up. Tip comes along and barks at all the neighbor dogs. I must be a pretty good rider or Mom and Dad wouldn't trust me to go alone.

If Mom and Dad aren't home, sometimes we ride the sows. We're not supposed to, but it isn't really dangerous. One of us goes down into the pasture and chases the old sows toward the chute. Only, you don't chase the boar. He has tusks. They're sort of like funny, long teeth. I mean *really* long, coming out of the side of his jaw. You just don't let him scare you. The rest of us stay up near the cement where the sows get fed. When they get going through the chute, we just drop on their backs and try to stay on 'til they get to the feeder shelf. That's the cement flat where they get fed at night. See, it's really not very scary. The sows can't turn around in the chute. If you fall off, get out of the way really quick, though, and try not to fall in the mud. There's a lot of you-know-what in it. And Mom will smell that we've been down here.

I am waiting outside the bedroom. That's where they're having the meeting. The boys' club does stuff together. Mostly they build stuff, like tree houses. They are voting on whether I can belong. I'm not really worried, but it feels sort of funny to be voted on. They don't vote whether boys can join.

It's sort of lonely 'cause the only other girl lives five miles away. Well, no, there's Janice. But she can't ride a horse. We always have to play inside. Janice is real good at tea and books, but I'm not very good at playing tea. Sometimes we go up to her bedroom and look at new books. She reads a lot. Really a lot. I don't really like books, 'cept if they have a lot of pictures or if they show you how to do something. Janice is really smart. There's just me and her in grade two. She is always first. Her mom teaches her at home some. I think my mom says Janice's mom is "over-protective" 'cause she was "older" when Janice was born. I'm not sure what that means, but I think it means Janice isn't ever going to learn to ride a horse.

Nels opens the door to the bedroom. Tom and Dave are on the edge of the bed. Chris is on the floor. Airie is sitting on the chair. "Okay, you're in. You're the architect."

- - - - - -

"What do you mean I can't sleep out there?" I can tell there is no point in arguing with my mom, but it doesn't feel fair to help build it and then not be able to sleep in it. I worked hard on that tree house.

"Is it 'cause Nels cut my lip when he was teaching me to notch the trees? He was really sorry. It didn't hurt much."

"No, it's not that. That was an accident."

"Well, then what?"

"There are just too many boys."

"So what?"

"The answer is NO."

"It isn't fair."

"You're right. It isn't. But that doesn't change my answer."

Home economics is compulsory. And it's boring. All girls in grade seven have to learn to make button holes and slip stitch and make muffins. I have been making suppers since grade four, and I made my first dress (with Mom's help) in grade six. Sometimes I ask if I can just stay home all day and go riding. Mom seems to understand. I take a lunch: eight oatmeal cookies, three or four plums, a peanut-butter-and-jam sandwich (plus an extra one for Tip), and some carrots for Lady. I put it all in a plastic bag and tie it to my belt loop. I pull Lady up to the dog house. If I stand on top of the dog house, I can usually get Lady close enough to jump on with three or four tries. Dad never lets us use a saddle after Nels got dragged 'cause he cinched it up wrong. So now we always have to find another way to get on.

It's five miles to the "fairy ring." No one else knows where it is. I found it accidentally. You have to follow just the right path to find it in the woods. You can ride right along side of it and never notice. I know there are no such things as fairies, but if there were, that's where they would dance. I never feel lonely in the fairy ring. Lady reins. That means she stands pretty still if you just drop her rein. She won't go far away. I have to chew the knot on my lunch bag open. Tip gets his sandwich and Lady gets her carrots. They seem to like having lunch with me. The oatmeal cookies taste better smashed. It's just me and the fairy ring. No yesterday. No tomorrow. Just today. Just quiet. It is someplace where I don't really do anything. I just watch. And listen. I don't really think about anything — 'cept maybe how to get back on Lady. Sometimes I feel like I'm not alone. I feel real quiet inside.

It is a beautiful day in May, 1964. One of those days that takes spring a whole week further from winter. It's a Friday. I am home from school because I am sick. I am nearly better, and I am bored.

"Why don't you walk down and get the mail? It will do you good."

Tip comes with me, and he chases the rocks I kick. I keep thinking about Freeman. I wish I could visit him. They say he is really sick. Freeman is the choir director. I am the pianist. He is special. He taught me to play crib, and he always stops his work when I walk over to his farm for hot chocolate. He is only forty-six, and he is dying. No one really says that, but I know. I stop just between the two sloughs. I kind of pray: "Give him back to us, even if it's only for a few days. Give him back, and I will do something to help." I pick up a rock, far too round, and try to skip it across the water. It plunks. Tip and I hurry a bit because I don't want the kids on the school bus to see me. There is nothing in the mail that looks very interesting. I set it on the kitchen table. Mom is standing at the phone. There are tears in her eyes.

"They are bringing him home. He wants to die being able to see the big tree."

I know how beautiful the big tree is. The bargain, in my mind, has been struck.

His bedroom is just off the living room. As I enter, his head turns toward me. He looks much older than the Freeman I know. He has lost so much weight, and his face is drawn. He doesn't have teeth that really fit. It was having his teeth out that started the bleeding, the bleeding that led to the diagnosis, the diagnosis that is his death warrant.

I come often. I just sit here. The time is special. Today Freeman seems to want to talk. I just listen. He's telling me about family: "Family is all any of us really have. You need to know your family. All of them, not just your one branch. I bet you don't even know the names of my brothers." I nod my head. He is right. I don't know. I know he's my dad's cousin, I think.

"Promise me you will take an interest in your family tree." With another nod, I promise.

We talk like I have never talked with an adult before. When Freeman talks, his mouth gets very dry. It's like his cheeks stick to his tongue. On my lap I have a bowl full of tiny ice cubes the size of miniature marshmallows. I slip them in the side of his mouth. I had been visiting often, so I have developed a sense of when he needs one. Today he seems to want me to stay longer. For the first time he says openly, "I will miss you."

"I'll miss you, too." I am surprised I have no tears. I am not sure I even feel sad. I just feel close. He gives me that smile that I was used to when I was playing the piano faster than the choir could sing. As if he needs to tell me something but he knows I might not necessarily play any differently.

"I have regrets, you know. Don't let yourself have a lot of regrets."

"How do I avoid it?"

"Live every day so that when you go to sleep at night, it would be okay if this were the last day of your life."

I never forgot.

We are burying Grandpa today. It's foggy outside. Not cold for this time of year, just very foggy. The news of his death is no surprise, but I feel strange as I look at his Christmas present all wrapped and ready to go. Every Christmas we say, "We are lucky to have Grandpa for another Christmas." This year there will be no Grandpa sitting in the recliner, half opening his gifts, then wrapping them up again while he watches the activity of the room.

I am aware of being watched: I am part of the bereaved family. I feel alone as I sit here. I want a hand to hold. I am composed, though. But I am struggling with this service. Why is the minister droning on about Jesus and Pharisees and pearly gates and not about Grandpa? Grandpa was not about parables and Pharisees.

I wish they hadn't taken away his wrinkles. With his eyes closed, he lacks the character that is so much him. Just days before, his ninety-five-year-old eyes had twinkled with delight when he asked, "Did you bring any candy?" The black suit they have put on him is so out of keeping. For years he's worn a Norwegian sweater. Why not bury him in his Norwegian sweater? I am reminded of my dream last night:

> It is a warm, autumn afternoon. It is Grandpa's funeral. It is being held in a gymnasium, and Grandpa is seated in a chair below the stage. As the proceedings begin, he stirs to aliveness and, in his teetering yet quick step, exits by the left aisle. Before anyone collects their thoughts, he has disappeared in the the nearby woods. A brief search yields nothing.
>
> Dad is concerned: "What if he doesn't find his way?"
>
> I am calm "There are several clear paths, Dad. He will be okay."

My mind comes back to the proceedings. The procession past his body is beginning. I silently say my thank yous: Thank you, Grandpa, for my dad . . . for making it possible for me to grow up on a farm . . . for always having raspberry drops in your glove compartment . . . for sipping wine behind Grandma's back . . . for trying to teach me Norwegian. I find myself stopping at the coffin. I whisper, "Good-bye, Grandpa." There is a tear — an okay tear.

I am a grandmother now. A young grandmother, but a grandmother. Grandmothers are supposed to die before their grandsons. I feel so powerless. Shiloh was born on September 7th. I only saw him twice. At some level I had fantasized being important to that little guy. The last time I fed him and held him, I said to him, "You have a whole story to tell me with your eyes." And he did. His little face wrinked and squirmed an epic from behind his near-black eyes. He lived thirty-seven days. He died on Thanksgiving morning of Sudden Infant Death Syndrome. When John, our son by choice, called, I felt hit where I had never been hit before.

Between the sobbing John pleaded, "Mom, what more do I have to do? I've been straight. I've been doing real good. Why Shiloh? Why Shiloh?"

I had no answers. I didn't know how to answer his letter that came later. I could hardly deal with my pain. How could I begin to help him deal with his? I read and reread his letter:

> Since I have lost Shiloh . . . there is nothing. Everything is so, so trivial. I don't fear death myself now. I find myself thinking, "Okay, Lord . . . I've honestly had it. This world is the shits . . . Take me now, please." I would never take my life or cause my death, Mom. Please understand that . . . but also understand that I'm sick and tired and believe even my own hope is gone. I know there will ·be a tomorrow, and a next week, and a next month, but right now all I have and see is today. I know these feelings are part of my mourning, and yet I feel when I'm older and dying I will not fear it. I will grasp it, relish it, accept it, and go on to my son. I know I gotta go on. I can give names of people I love, and I know I owe it to the ones in my life to keep going. For Rosemary, for Ashley, you, Dad, Delores, Twyla, and myself, but mostly for my son . . . I will go on. I promise, no matter how much I really don't want to. I'm just so tired.

What do I say to my son? How do I speak to him of hope?

When I die, Irene will be the one who speaks for me. She has already been my friend for thirty years. We are sisters by choice. She is a doer. She doesn't talk about problems; she solves them. She doesn't talk about helping; she helps. I know if I phone, she will come. I know if I hurt, she will comfort. Not necessarily pamper, but comfort. She will draw my strength to my awareness. And we laugh together. At nothing. Just take joy in laughing.

She will do my eulogy. Not because she wants to but because she knows me. And she will honor the parts of me that are important. And she will reminisce, about our first hunting trip: how she nearly shot me and how she was stupid enough to go into a slough that had been crapped in all summer by purebred herefords to retrieve a duck I had shot. And she will tell how I stood, with a straight face, on the water's edge, giving directions. How she fell, pink angora sweater and all, the victim of a twisted foot in the slough bed. How I broke into fits of laughter as she continued to slug her way to the evidence of my marksmanship. All on a cold October day.

And she will smile as she tells of how I seduced her to plunge into a mountain lake in early May. She who is a good swimmer and me who can only dog paddle. How she didn't know that, before coming down the hundred steps to the glacier lake to take the plunge, I had run a tub to the brim with hot water. And how on the same trip we took three days to approach a nestling loon. And she will speak of the patience it took to get the picture. It hangs in her home.

She will speak of our connectedness. Of our shared memories. Of the memories that make us family.

The Voice of School

A CHILD OF HOPE ASSUMES THAT THE WORLD is the same for every child. That all that is necessary is to keep risking, keep trusting, keep loving. But at some point the innocence of that hope meets the realities of the world. If we are fortunate, our hope is nestled deep in our spirit before the assaults begin. If it is, the thread of hope that is the continuity of life is never severed. It is pulled taut and strengthened.

School teaches us hope in disparate ways. For those with ability and opportunity, it affirms our worth and opens doors to our future. We learn to read and to write and to lead. When we notice all is not equal, we have the invitation to learn to act on behalf of tolerance and cooperation. Our hope grows up. We discover that hope is not something that we can keep for ourselves. We begin to notice that hope is tied to justice.

Hoping is noticing the injustices, too. Acting on them. Not always winning. Learning more with each effort. Being open to change. Even being thankful the system isn't perfect. Hoping is

appreciating that we can act. Hope is learning that errors are teachers, too. Hope is understanding that we all are learners and all teachers. That we need each other to deepen and mature our hope.

The education system extends our awareness of the dichotomies of life: of rich and poor, of strong and weak, of the marginalized and the preferred, of success and failure, of cooperation and competition, of leading and following, of knowing scientifically and knowing by intuition. Most of all, of inequity and justice.

When I first started out in school, the one-room school I attended was like a family. We cared about each other. We had to. There wasn't even a ball team unless everyone played together. When I was older, the larger school I went to was a larger window into life. Into hope. It wasn't hard to figure out that there were more opportunities if you were smart and if you were of "good stock." I felt awkward at times with intelligence and athletic prowess and Caucasian parents. Schoolwork came relatively easy for me. I was naturally blessed with the capacity to be disciplined. I was quickly made the team captain, the class representative, the student council president. The discipline to do well was a thirst to understand.

My strongest memories, though, are not of the trophies or the achievements but of the inequities over which I had little control. Of the classmates who had little power to learn or to influence their lives. Of wondering why intuition and hunches were unacceptable and feelings irrelevant. The indelible imprints are not of the delight of learning but of the oppression of rarely being asked to think.

Yet I am grateful for the experience of school. Grateful for the love and opportunities that were mine by chance. Thankful that my cast was well set prior to school; that I was athletic and intellectually able; that I was seldom ridiculed. Grateful for the teachers who challenged and helped. Grateful for the ones who made me reach inside to seek my own truth.

Later, as a teacher myself, I was grateful for the students who were the mirrors of my inadequacies; grateful for the ones who encouraged me to believe in change and growth. They all invited me to know that teaching is about caring. And caring sets the stage for hope.

It's the last day of school. All we are doing is playing ball 'til noon. I love ball, but I'm glad it's summer holidays. We can play ball lots in the summer. I passed to grade two. It wasn't very hard. I'm pretty smart. Not as smart as Julie, though.

School's okay. There is just one room for all six grades, and I like that. In grade one there are just two of us. Grade oners get to sit by the stove first in the morning. I like sitting by the stove. You can even keep your mitts on.

I like some stuff, but the teacher makes you do a lot of things the hard way. I would rather be riding Lady. Or helping Mom. When I finish my lessons, I can listen in on the others. Or read. Most of the stories are pretty dumb, though. The teacher is always saying, "Take home a book and read it to your mom and bring back the piece of paper that says you read it to her." She doesn't say Mom has to listen to it. My mom listens but the stories are pretty boring, even for me.

I like going to a one-room school 'cause everybody gets to play together. Nobody gets left out. We can only play ball with teams when everybody plays, and even then we only have two fielders. Julie is up to bat. Julie gets four strikes. She is as old as I am, but she doesn't hit so good. She's really smart at books, but she needs four strikes. Everyone knows Julie gets four strikes. And that's okay. I'm not so good at spelling.

There are a lot more kids at the big school. I know most of them. This is my second year here. Mom went back to teaching last year, so we go to this school now. The school bus takes over an hour to get here, but we ride with Mom.

Fran just came this year. She has a soft, kind of shy smile and really blond hair that is naturally wavy. I think she is kind of pretty, but she gets teased a lot. Maybe it's her glasses. They are really thick, and they made her blue eyes look extra big. And she's real shy. One day I was talking to her and she said, "I wish I knew why you won't be my friend." I felt bad, more like awkward. I didn't even know she wanted me to be her friend. I guess I sort of accidentally ignored her. It is hard 'cause I always play ball at noons and recesses. I don't really know how to be a friend with someone who is shy and doesn't play ball. She seems to feel okay just knowing I like her and that I like having her on my team when everybody has to play ball.

It feels really good to be asked to her birthday. My mom bought a cake and had Fran's name put on it. Mom drove us all to Fran's house on an acreage. I didn't know Fran didn't have a mom. Her dad is nice, though. He looks so tired. Maybe that's how dads get when they try to raise five kids alone. They don't have much money. No wonder Fran looks like some of the orphans.

We are having a wonderful walk. It's one of those days when you just never want to go inside 'cause its so nice. There is a little breeze, but you don't need a sweater and its light out 'til real late. We walk in a line down the rutted road. They have two dogs that keep running around us.

Fran says quietly, "We're moving."

"Where?"

"I don't know."

We walk in silence. I wish I knew where they are moving next. They are always moving. Fran seems sad.

I'm glad we're not moving.

We were supposed to "write an essay about what you want to be when you grow up." I wrote about wanting to be a 'sykyatrist.' I know what they do, and I know how long they have to go to school. And I know you have to be pretty smart to get to be one.

Mom teaches in the next room. I am cleaning the boards at the far end of the room. That's my job while I wait for Mom after school. It takes her a while to plan the next day and to gather up everything she has to take home. She takes lots of stuff home every night. Mrs. H. is talking to her – real loud. She knows I can hear.

"Read your daughter's essay."

Mom takes the notebook. I walk up to the front of the room and wait for her eyes to tell me if I did okay. Mrs. H. looks down at me and then looks at Mom. Mrs. H. is always stern. If you look around in class, she comes up behind and raps you on the head with the edge of her wedding ring.

"She says she wants to be a psychiatrist, and she can't even spell it."

I can feel something die in me. Mom is giving her back my notebook and speaking to me, but I don't hear anything. I didn't know I couldn't be a 'sykyatrist.' I thought I could do anything. I have a feeling like when I fell playing dodge ball and got the wind knocked out of me. Except I feel bad, too. How many other things can't I do?

Miss T. doesn't really like kids. Especially if they are poor. Mrs. H. was grumpy, but at least she treated all the kids the same. Miss T. hardly ever speaks to Donald or Marvin. They are Metis. I think their mom is native and their dad is white, but I don't know for sure. And I don't think they have the same dad. They're from the orphanage. They have to sit right at the front. Funny, 'cause she treats them like they don't even exist. Donald slouches a lot, and his shoulders are kind of rounded, like someone who is a grandparent already. He never looks at anyone. Marvin has a really neat smile, but he kind of cringes sometimes. He's a good ball player, though, especially at short stop. But he hardly ever says anything.

It isn't so much what she says. It's the way she says it. She doesn't say things *to* them. She talks *about* them, so that we all know that she thinks they are less. It makes me feel smaller. I feel ashamed. Nobody says anything. I don't know what to say. I just know what she does is wrong. I wonder what makes people do things like that. I know she wouldn't do those things to me. I feel badly and grateful at the same time.

We celebrate Christmas on Christmas Eve. There is lots to eat, and there are tons of presents under the tree. Well, at least three for each person. We eat lutefish because Dad is Norwegian, but we eat Christmas pudding for dessert because Mom is English. Mary's Christmas is very different from mine.

Mary walks up the old lake bank road, no matter what the weather, to catch the school bus. On Sunday she walks even further to come to Sunday School. You can't even drive down the road. I have been down to her house once, and I can remember staring at the walls in her bedroom because the boards weren't close enough to shut out light. I could feel the breeze on an autumn day. I wondered how she could sleep there in the winter. My room is original log covered with plaster board, but there aren't any cracks. And my mom always puts a hot water bottle in the bed before bedtime. I know Mary's mom doesn't.

I wasn't riding the bus that morning. I am glad I wasn't. The school bus just about drove over her mom. She was frozen right into the snow. They say she and her husband walked home. He made it. She didn't. I knew that there was something wrong with that. Some other kids on the bus once told me about the time their dad put manure in their Christmas stockings, but this is a lot worse. Mary's mom died. Mary wouldn't even have a mom for Christmas.

There are books from floor to ceiling on the back wall and only one free-standing shelf, nearly to the ceiling. I come here often because it beats sitting at my desk. I'm always finishing my assignments early, so my teacher always says, "You can go to the library." The library is a lonely place. No one else is finished with their work, so my choices are to be bored at my desk or to be bored at the library.

I like books with ideas. In grade eight they want you to read stories. Pages and pages of description that just bores me. I liked reading Darwin. Now that guy had ideas. I loved doing my science report. And some of the poetry is neat. The problem with being finished early isn't being in the library alone; it's not that most of the books aren't what I like. It's that when I read a book, there is no one to talk to about it. I get lonely. I wonder if anyone else likes thinking.

Sometimes, if I am restless, Miss T. says, "Get out your books and study until the other children are ready." Sometimes I study really hard. I even give up riding and stay home from volleyball. I have to study a lot because the exams are weird. Sometimes I sit and doodle while I figure out the questions. Some of the questions are easy. Some of them are hard because if you really think about the question, there could be more than one answer. It just says pick the *best* answer. Well, that depends a lot on how you see the question. I know my teacher will say there is only one right answer. And final exams count for so much. How come the year's work doesn't count? They keep saying school is like work. Well, I don't see teachers having everything depend on one day. When I am a teacher, I'm sure not going to give my students multiple-choice exams.

I am almost twenty, and it's my first year as a teacher. My portable classroom can get pretty cold. The back door opens and a breeze notifies me of a visitor. It's the principal. I don't hear him even knock. He is a tall man with tall nose and a wide mustache. He's slim and narrow, and so are his eyes. He stands right at my desk and says loudly, "Where is Steven? Do you know where Steven is?"

I stand up. "No. Why?"

"You don't know where Steven is?"

"No."

"Well, he is downtown, and you haven't reported him as absent."

"Well, he isn't supposed to be in my room right now."

"He is downtown." His voice is getting louder. The students are watching with interest. I feel like I am being reprimanded right in front of my class.

"It is your responsibility to know where your students are." With that he leaves the room as abruptly as he entered.

I sit down. The students sit quietly. I rise. Out the door, across the snow, down the long hall, to the principal's office. I stand. I am afraid I will lose my nerve if I sit down. There is only a momentary wait. Mrs. C. says, "You can go in now."

I choose a wooden chair with arms. I sit on the edge. He sits, his pen still in his hand, still poised over his paper as if I would be only a moment in his day. I take a tense breath and say, "I may not know some things, but I know that how you dealt with me in my classroom is not acceptable."

My words stop with his interruption. His "you're-a-rookie, you-have-a-lot-to-learn" lecture starts. I am determined to be heard. I interrupt. "The student was not scheduled to be in my room. And you were rude." I decide not to wait for a second lecture and, without raising my voice, end with, "When you can speak to me like I am a person, I will listen."

I leave. All the way down the hall I am thinking, "Where am I going to work next year?" He never bugs me again.

Terri is one of the brightest, most athletic girls in my eighth grade class. What is happening with her? I don't know what I am going to say to her. But it's worth trying. She plunks herself on the second desk back, waiting for a a lecture. I try to ask questions.

"Terri, is something wrong these days?"

"Why?"

"Well, you don't seem your old self."

"What do you mean?" Her voice is resentful.

"Well, you used to care about your marks and your looks."

"That's my business."

"Well, yes, it is but I care."

Her eyes drop a little.

"Is that all?"

"I guess. I wish there was something I could say or do."

Silence.

"Can I go now?"

I stand at my desk. I know I have lost contact with her. I know she feels judged. How should I have said it? I don't know.

Dale is a superb young female athlete. She's a good kid with a wonderful sense of humor. For the most part we get along well. The only problem is she is so cocky, it is near impossible to teach her anything. I am her physical education teacher. She is unquestionably the best badminton player in grade eight. She is interested in winning, not in getting better. She can whip anyone in her class, and she knows it. I put her on the other side of the net from me. I seat the class around the court. She doesn't know I have played in the Canadian school girl championships. Her face smirks with the opportunity to beat the teacher. I not only score on her, I practically make her eat the birdie with every point. She runs from side to side and from back to front with increasing vengeance and then with increasing panic. The game ends. The score is 15-0.

"The next time I ask you to try something, maybe you will listen." I hadn't taught. I had broken. She didn't bend, she tolerated.

What else did I expect from humiliation?

The teachers' noon-hour patrol is a routine to force students to stay in their rooms for fifteen minutes and eat their lunches. I see Gerry shuffling down the hallway. Ah! A victim.

"You know the rules. What are you doing out here? Where is your lunch? You know better. I expect more. Now go and get your lunch."

He can't get a word in edgewise. He doesn't even try. His eyes stare at his shoes.

"Look at me when I talk to you." His eyes meet mine.

"I don't have a lunch."

Still indifferent, I press on. "Did you forget it?"

"No, there is no food in the house." His eyes tell me he is speaking the truth. I feel like crawling in the nearest key hole. All I can do is apologize and get him some lunch. When will I learn to give kids the benefit of the doubt? When will I learn that they aren't deliberately setting out to be difficult? That children have a right to hide their shame? How did keeping the hall clear of children get more important than listening to one who doesn't have a lunch?

And I thought I was going to make a difference in the lives of children. It isn't so easy to be "child oriented." I better start to figure out what I am hoping to do as a teacher.

This will be my first year as a counsellor. I am still young. As I approach the front counter, there are students leaning against it either getting or waiting for help. The secretary asks if I am there to register. I resolve to wear my hair in a bun for a few days, never thinking that my mini-skirt might have something to do with the youthful impression. There are three other full-time counsellors. Two are quiet and gently spoken. Ray, the department head, is a straight shooter whose language is more colorful than appreciated at times, at least by those accustomed to cultured conversation. I soon learn he isn't afraid of innovation or resistance. When I propose a new program, he supports me one hundred percent and then says, "But don't screw up." Kids come first on his list. If it helps kids, he is for it. He expects me to be competent. I wonder if he knows I have never taken a counselling course! Somehow, though, I have a sense I will fit here. I will make a difference here.

Marnee is tall, pushing six feet. For a girl, that's hard. It's even harder when you are from a screwball family, where you are allowed to eat only after the rest of the family has finished; where you are told you were never wanted; where you are told you are stupid. In reality Marnee is bright; she is hungry for love. For some reason, we hit it off. She starts to trust me. She starts doing better in classes like art. Not so in ones where she is supposed to sit quietly for fifty minutes.

Every once in a while she rages. She breaks everything she has made in pottery class except for two things she has made for me. The pencil holder and Jake. "Jake" sits on my bookshelf. Jake is a gnome-like figure with an orange hat. I found him on my desk one morning with a note that said, "Jake would like to come and live with you."

One day she "lost it" in class. Someone teases her. She comes into the guidance area yelling, "I'm going to get her." She has a knife. Thankfully, she complies with my command, "Marnee, give me the knife." She does so and runs past me into the school foyer and out the door. I don't know how a police car arrives. She is wrestled into it. I am left to wrestle with the questions. What kind of future is ahead for her? Is there really any hope for her? How much of a difference do we really make?

As counsellors, we don't see teachers as clients. Our mandate is to work with the kids. But it is easy to see that teachers have troubles, too. They aren't different from anyone else. Ted is a good teacher. Very thorough. Well liked. An introvert by nature, he has been been even more withdrawn lately. A colleague has pointed out to me that he might be seriously depressed. I have mentioned it to a counsellor colleague and to an administrator. The consensus is that it isn't really our business. There is a hint that, with experience, I will be able to sense what's appropriate to get involved in and what not to. They are probably right. Being so young, I probably don't have the credibility.

It is late Thursday afternoon. It's hot. I am heading home, listening to the radio. I am at Center Street and Memorial Trail when the news about the hostage taking comes on. There is a moment of awareness. That's near where Ted lives. "No, it can't be him." But it is.

Now Ted is dead. And I live not knowing if any of us could have made a difference. The lesson of inaction lingers a long time. If there was any hope, we missed it. We didn't act.

Harry is so grubby. I can hardly stand the smell when he is in my little office. He has more acne on one face than a record case of measles. Most of the pimples ooze. He loves automotives, and he takes a personal interest in keeping my car serviced in the school shop. His spirits are always up. He comes to see me because I am his academic adviser, but each time we talk, he shares a bit about his home. One day I inquire, "Harry, you talk about your dad a lot but not about your mom? Where is she in your life?"

"Oh, she's on the mantle."

"On the mantle?"

"Yeah, she died a couple of years ago, and dad and I, we got her on the mantle. There is just me and my dad now. He doesn't cook so good. I get up at five and make him breakfast and start the car so he doesn't have to go outside into a cold car. Then I go back to bed. That's why I'm late sometimes. I sleep in."

I hate being asked to talk to Harry about his smell.

"Yes, um, Mrs. F." He never sits down. He just stands waiting, expecting to be asked to change the oil in my car.

"Harry, we know each other pretty good, don't we?"

"Sure."

"Harry, can I be straight with you?"

"Sure."

"Harry, how often do you bathe?"

"Sometimes once a week."

"Harry, would you be willing to try something?"

"Sure."

"Would you bathe maybe three times a week?"

"Ah, okay, but why?"

"Harry, some of us have noticed that the grease smell stays with you."

"Oh, okay."

And he does. And his acne improves.

I first see Jim for absenteeism. He's a wiry kid. Masculine but small. He's honest, up front about the priorities in his life. And he's on a list for possible expulsion.

"Jim, you have missed a lot of school."

"Yeah, I know. Am I going to get kicked out?"

"I don't know. Is there anything that we should know that would help us understand?"

"No, I don't think so." His voice is non-defensive.

"Well, has anything unusual been happening lately? Anything that makes it difficult to get to school?"

"Well, kind of. Dad died, so I have to get the truck sold before it's repossessed. Sis is in the drug scene in Vancouver, so I had to go get her. My other sister is havin' a baby, and her man is in the slammer, so there are some things I gotta do. I make most of my spending money for the year from selling Christmas trees, so I had to get that set up. But not much other than that."

"Let me think about this, Jim. Can you tell me, though, do you want to go to school?"

"Well, ya. But I got other stuff to do, too."

"Makes sense to me."

I check it out. If anything, Jim has understated things. His dad committed suicide.

And we were calling this kid a loser.

The Voice of Intimacy

The longing is such that one might seek solace in friendships or in the perfect marriage – but it is never enough. And yet even if it were enough, a second issue arises – it will not last.[2]

THE HOPE FOR INTIMACY IS THE HOPE TO SATISFY a longing: the unnamed longing that we sense lies in a relationship of trust and companionship and caring. That hope is the adult version of our real or imagined mothers of hope and families of hope. The hope for an intimate relationship is the hope for someone to be present in our lives. Someone who will listen. Someone who likes and loves us, despite our shortcomings. Who shares our dreams. To whom we can be known in a way that we are not known to the others in our world. With whom we can be

---

2 W. Paul Jones, *Theological Worlds.* Nashville: Abington Press, 1989, p. 47.

vulnerable. Who won't go away. Someone with whom we will share the pain and joy, the valleys and the peaks of our lives. It is the experience of coming home. To somewhere where we belong. We can be there by invitation only; it can only happen mutually.

Hoping for intimacy means risking and learning. Risking being our own person. Risking letting another be their own person. Risking rejecting and being rejected. Risking again. Learning to heal. Learning to choose healing. Risking staying open to the pain so we can heal. Learning to stay open to love so we can grow. Risking being alone. Learning to choose aloneness at times. Learning the power of choice. Risking being responsible for our choices.

Fulfilling the hope for intimacy is about choosing freedom *and* commitment. Learning that when and if it happens, it brings responsibility. It is about being there, being open. It is about risking and learning to be "present," without losing self. Hoping for intimacy is learning about love, however the lessons are packaged.

Our culture indoctrinates us with the hope of the ideal

relationship. Our longing is to be satisfied in a sole relationship. The match must be approved according to the dictates of our culture. The right age, the right status. Perhaps even the right gender. The popular psychology books presume to tell us how. The jargon of intimacy is a multimillion dollar business. Yet a relationship is not a matter of contracts and assertiveness and working out codependencies. It is the dynamic of the way in which we are "present" for the other. The hope lies in moving toward acceptance and maturity, forgiveness and good will, kindness and respect – in authenticity and humanness.

In our search for intimacy, we meet the dichotomies of acceptance and rejection, of ideal and human, of silence and communication, of individuality and compromise, of self and the other. In the space between, in the space where hope draws us forward, we meet joy and illusion; we struggle with possessiveness and freedom; we confront our capacity to choose. The longing and the hope take each of us on our own journey. For a few, the hope is fulfilled with ease. For others, it is a long and painful journey. For most of us, it is a pathway to maturity.

I married the prince who expected a storybook version of the princess. The marriage failed. It hurt. I healed. I risked again. I sold my car, resigned my job, and gave my notice to my landlord – I was leaving to begin a new life with a new partner in Arkansas. Only days before I was to leave, the phone call came cancelling that future. This time, the healing took longer.

Time passed. I risked again. This time, I was the one who did the hurting. I couldn't handle the unconventional. I couldn't make the jump. I chose aloneness. I had to learn that my hope was not someone else's responsibility. I had to learn to know and value my own companionship. But the longing didn't go away. Rather, I found for it a rightful place, a place where the aloneness would not overwhelm me.

Eventually, I chose a partner for life. Now, the longing is quieter. I am no longer recreating the family or community of my childhood. I am co-creating the place where I belong as an adult.

Today is my convocation day. Laurel is having a party for me after the formalities. Mom and Dad came early enough for the ceremonies. Gram and my aunt Fay are here, too. It would be fun if Ron could be here. He asked me on the phone last week, "What would you like for convocation?" I kidded, "A crazy Arkansan with a bow around his neck." I know that can't be. I feel no particular disappointment. That's just life. It is a special day, and I am going to focus on what is, not on what isn't.

Ron and I met at a workshop. One of those experiences where disclosure is part of the experience. Where people get close quickly. Where the realities of the world are distant for a few days. He was American. I was the 'canuck.' He was extroverted and somewhat burdened. I was introverted and free. He was thirteen years older and wrestling early with midlife. Our strength was that we could play. It's fun risking again. I had hurt for a long time after my divorce. It feels good to be valued, good to dream about a future. A future that may or may not be. Today it doesn't matter. I am here. He is there.

There is a good feeling as the crowd disperses and Dad takes the last picture. I feel like it is as much my parents' day as it is mine. They have good reason to be proud, good reason to share in my success. I love them. They have, in their quiet way, been there through the years of learning.

Back at the house I spot several of the cars I know to be friends'. I am pleased to see my graduate adviser's. I am ready to party. Laurel is the first to hug me as I come up the back steps into the kitchen. "Way to go! Folks are already here. Go on in."

I hear him at the same moment I see him. His Arkansan drawl is unmistakable: "I got my bow on." There Ron stands with the biggest red bow I had ever seen around his neck.

For a moment all is still. My eyes glaze with a would-be tear. The lump in my throat stops the words. I shake my head. "You are something else."

"So are you, Babe. Are you surprised?"

The element of surprise makes his leaving doubly hard. I am puzzled how he can be part of a beginning and not part of an ending. He leaves me to do the ending alone.

> When you said, "Come,"
> The tears
> Streamed down my face
> In the Arkansan rain.
> Tears of joy.
> Your love,
> God's wilderness
> And a chance to grow.
> What more
> Could there be?
>
> Then you went away.
>
> Why did you go away
> So suddenly
> Like an adolescent lad
> Raw with love,
> Flooded with questions?
>
> I can think
> Of nothing
> I have done
> To earn your silence.
>
> I find it difficult
> In your silence
> To confirm
> I am lovable.

The ending doesn't happen in a moment, or in a day. The flashes of *what was* keep getting mixed up with flashes of what *would have been.*

I traipse barefoot
To the laundry room
Clad in blue jeans
And the T-shirt
I've treasured
Since San Diego.
As I stuff
Dripping clothes
Through the dryer door,
I have a flash
Of disappointment:
There are none of yours
Mixed with mine.

Thoughts of you
Slip into my day
So unexpectedly.

I know: It takes time. But how long? Some days, the pain is momentary and eternal at the same time.

Sometimes
I wonder,
"Will I ever heal?"
I feel I am,
And then with
The slightest bump,
A passing thought,
A fantasy,
A memory,
The wound
Again is raw —
The pain,
A silent scream
For peace.
For acceptance
That you have chosen
To go away.

I am learning the rhythm of my own pain. Before I accept that I have choices, I have to accept that he also chooses. My powerlessness will not reverse his choice. He doesn't even know I am hurting.

I vacillate.
One moment I feel strong
Defiant to all forces —
The next,
Naked
Raw
Hurt
Unwilling to accept
I have a choice of feelings.

The healing will take a long time. Until then, I will find a rightful place for my woundedness. Some place that is honored and yet not vulnerable. At least not so very vulnerable.

I choose.
It is time
To put my heart in order.
To place you
In fond memories.
To open myself
For the love
Of others
Who might respond.

The evening sun is dipping behind the distant knoll of the English countryside. The irregular contours signal the nearness of the village. To the left, across a stream, a church steeple is a sentinel against a darkening sky. No doubt a storm is on its way. It is like the beginning of a Dickens' story. The wind has picked up. Peddling my bike is harder than ever.

I haven't been well today. Pain has become a routine night visitor, as has the nausea and often the vomiting. As long as I don't eat much, I do okay. Glen has noticed, but we don't talk much about it. What is there to say? The symptoms have been there for months before the bicycle trip. We've been doing fine. A few miles a day. Stop for a ploughman's lunch. Meet the locals. It's been great, except sometimes it's such an effort. And this headwind isn't helping. The power of my downward stroke moves me only minusculey along the roadside.

Glen, a hundred yards ahead, sees I am making little headway. He turns back toward me. We both get off our bikes.

"Tough going. Bit weary?"

"Yeah."

"Like a little tow?"

I smile, but I don't really know what he means until he opens the bike pack and takes out a length of multi-purpose cord. In his quiet way he slips it on the bar of my bike and over to his. He smiles.

"How about we do it as a team?"

"Thanks."

He pulls away and with a little jerk as the rope goes taut, we are on our way. Mostly under his power, but with my strength doubled by his caring.

I enjoy the permission we share. Our sense of just being together.
There is a lot to be said for compatibility as a starting place.

> There is no concern
> Who pays for what
> Or where to go.
> It's sufficient to be going.

> There is no concern
> Who builds the fire,
> Who fries the steaks,
> Or makes the tea . . .

> He's cutting wood now.
> I'm writing.
> Neither has sought permission.
> Sharing,
> But not imposing.
> A quiet contract.

I can feel the invitation to be fully alive again. It is happening slowly. It's happening without words. And it feels good.

My friend and I are talking.
He stops.
Smiles.
I know words are too simple
So I smile back
And he understands.

But I want him to know
That I am reawakening a part of me
That I had put away
Because it hurt so much
To risk and lose.

The part of me that laughs
Had nearly died —
Trying to
To be acceptable
To someone
Who didn't understand
It hurt to stop laughing.

I resurrected it once
And was hurt yet again.
For a long time
It felt like the only way to live
Was to be
Alone.

Sometimes life is challenging enough without a set of rules for relationships. Being together isn't always possible. It helps having someone in my life who knows that.

What makes a friend a special friend?
Knowing, accepting there are gaps —
Gaps of experience, gaps of time,
Gaps of need, gaps of desire,
Yet wanting to share,
Feeling free to share.
Not expected to be 'this' or 'that.'
Just expected to be.

What makes a friend a special companion?
Knowing, accepting that each has limited time for the other —
That days are filled with living,
With relating to others,
With work.
Knowing, accepting that joy and sadness
Are shared with others —
And feeling not left out.

It takes a long time to risk again. I seem to take mini-steps. I am noticing how I disguise my caution with my language.

I've made such an effort to stay objective,
Not to say "I love you."
I've said,
With concern, "I care."
With joy, "You're beautiful!"
With appreciation, "It's great to hear from you."
With affection, "You're special."

I've been so careful to express
That my demands of you are few.
Mainly, be yourself.
And if that someday excludes me,
I can accept that.

I have been cautious in expressing
That there are moments,
Some longer than others,
Some endless,
When I love you.

There is no way of knowing the rightness of my choices. Sometimes I cannot even explain them. Even if I could, it wouldn't stop the pain. The gap between the wish and the reality still hurts.

Will the pain ever stop?
Will you ever be someone that I used to love?

Will the day come
   When I awake wanting to touch another?
Will I ever mount Telemachus
   And not miss you cycling on Ulysses?

Will I ever again
   Make angels in the snow,
      Be free to laugh?
         Or want to see the Eiffel tower again?

Will I ever feel
   My choice was right for me?
Or will I always live
   Wondering, What if?
   Thinking, If only?

Will the pain ever stop?
Will you ever be someone that I used to love?
I sometimes think we tried to do it by the book.
I wish I'd yelled
   or cried   or threatened
   or fallen madly in love   or had an affair
So you could
   yell   or cry   or threaten

But we didn't.
I guess we couldn't.
The scary part is, I don't know even know
If we could have done it differently.

Here I am alone again. Writing. Using my head to figure out my life. Struggling with my ambivalence, yet trying to honor it. It's hard not being with Glen. I'm trying to work out on paper who I am. A journal is not a life companion. But it is a companion. I have to smile at myself. It's as if I believe I will get more insight if I use a quill pen rather than a ball-point. If I write on parchment rather than in a notebook. If I drive out into nature, like today, rather than write in my stuffy apartment. It is more like a cell. It's a sweat house in the summer.

I am sitting here alone beside Elbow Falls. The aloneness feels okay. I am beginning to understand what they mean when they say you have to be your own best friend before you can be someone else's. I love the sound of the waterfall. It shuts out the sounds of the city. It reminds me of something primitive. Like what might have been before we had language. This is my favorite rock. It towers over the largest eddy just below the falls. I feel here a bit like I felt in the fairy ring when I was a child. I feel an intimacy with the universe. An intimacy with myself.

I am learning where I feel okay with my aloneness: I feel most alone in a crowd; I feel least alone in nature. I see a butterfly trying to get my attention. Butterflies only live for two weeks. Yet, they are so beautiful, so fragile. My pen begins to move.

> Is all my choosing illusion?
> Some moments I feel driven
> By a force beyond myself —
> Not like a God,
> More like a rhythm,
> Like a tide.
> I feel a "pull" from the unknown.
>
> Yet a caterpillar does not aspire
> To become a butterfly.
> An egg does not think
> To become a bird.
> Pollen does not decide
> To blossom a flower.
>
> Left natural,
> What would I become?

I'm not sure I like this idea of being responsible for my own life. It seems so hard to measure the consequences. I'm not sure if I want or don't want a road map.

Each day I am called upon
To create my own life.
Therein lies
Both an excitement
And a fear.
For if I choose my path,
I become
Responsible
For my journey.

If I choose
A path
Less traveled,
There will be
  fewer signposts
  fewer people
  fewer certainties
  fewer havens.
In exchange
There will be
  more mountains to climb
  more waters to ford
  more seasons to experience
  more quiet in my deep down.
How will I know if I have chosen well?

I agreed to go for lunch. That seemed low risk enough. A Saturday brunch date. I am not sure I have the energy for a relationship right now. My recent illness seems to have taken so much out of me. I'm not sure what I want. I like Allen, though. He has a wonderful laugh. He is very much a gentleman, and he seems determined to court me.

The buzzer signals that he is downstairs – early.

"Come on up. Just take the elevator to the twentieth floor and come in when you get here." I prop open the door so he can come in when he arrives. In a few minutes I hear the door open. I slip out to the living room to greet him.

"I'll just be a few minutes. You don't look well. Are you okay?"

"I am just tired."

"Why don't you put your head down? I'll be a few minutes."

"Maybe I will."

I am uneasy without knowing why. I tidy up the kitchen to give him a few extra minutes to rest. My galley kitchen is the classic eight-foot apartment version adjacent to the living room. I put my head around the corner. His color doesn't seem right.

"Are you sure you are okay? Should I call someone?"

"I'll be fine."

A few minutes later I find I am asking again: "Are you sure you are okay?"

"You better call someone."

"Who?"

"9-1-1."

The paramedics arrive literally in minutes. My apartment is across from the hospital. I have never watched a rescue team before. A dozen things are happening at once. Allen is conscious but hurting. Trying to cooperate. The paramedic team soon realizes that asking me questions about his history is not useful. Time seems to have stopped. At some point he is on the stretcher, and we are all headed for the elevator. The cargo elevator won't come up. One fellow says, "Okay, we'll do it the hard way."

The others seem to understand. As the narrow passenger elevator door opens, the first fellow says, "Now."

The stretcher is almost vertical. No one speaks. Everyone grins. Even Allen. Outside I find myself getting into the ambulance. As they settle him in, I find myself kidding him: "If this is about lunch, I would have paid." He smiles through the pain.

Ironically, they are taking us to a hospital across the city where his doctor practices. At the Emergency Room, the admitting attendant stops me and asks that I provide the necessary paper work. Little does she know: I don't even know where he lives. The response she gets is, "I will be back to do the paper work when I know he feels safe."

Much to my surprise, no one hassles me. A minute or two later, a nurse suggests I wait outside the treatment room.

"Thank you, but I am fine. He will feel safer if I am here."

Allen nods. I stay. His hand reaches out. I know he is thankful for the support. What I don't know is that this is the moment when he decides that I am the woman he wants in his life.

Risking again is hard. At one level, I know risking is the only way back to loving. At another level, I am wondering, "What am I doing?" I stand alone in my hotel room. I had promised myself that I would not go ahead if I didn't feel right about it, no matter what the social awkwardness. There is only a thread of hesitancy. But it tugs deeply. I suddenly become aware of Mom at the door.

"You okay, sis?" Mom's voice is assuring. Her look, understanding. She senses my thoughtfulness. Without words, we both know the moment has come. I appreciate that there is no pep talk. No advice.

"I'm okay. I just hope I'm not making another mistake."

There is an accepting smile. We head out the door. Allen is waiting. We give Mom time to get to her place on the lawn. The August sun beats down. Before I know it, the minister is reading the entrée we had written to our vows. We begin alternating, as we had practiced a hundred times as we committed them to memory. Suddenly, the guests fall away and the most intimate moments of my life begin.

I feel gentle. Allen is asleep only minutes after lunch. Strange how we have a relationship even as he lies there. I am as close as if we were snuggling in bed, having what has become our ritual late at night: talking in the dark — about the kids, about how lucky we are, how time is running out for us, how we want to write with the time we have, how it beats golfing our way through retirement, how The Hope Foundation will be a lot of work, how it is also the work that gives meaning to our lives.

I love being with a companion who talks. When I used to go for long walks with Tip, I had only the wag of his tail by which to measure his interest in any given gopher hole.

The late night talks are never over until Allen says, "It will be okay." I feels like he says it differently every night. The way I need to hear it *that* night. He doesn't know it, but I let myself sense whatever I might be concerned about, and when he says, "It will be okay," I let myself believe it will be.

I love feeling safe. And not judged. My heart gets bigger, and I know I can take on just a little more than I could just minutes before. I know from how his head bows to mine, like a tall adolescent boy who doesn't want to be too forward, that we are a team. That whatever it is, we will do it together. Freely.

I drift off to sleep with my head on his left shoulder. Sooner or later I somehow end up on my pillow.

The Voice of Illness

ILLNESS IS AN INTRODUCTION TO THE FRAGILITY and sacredness of life. With illness we learn we are not immune. Nor are those whom we love. We learn that our sense of invulnerability is an illusion. Illness is the great equalizer. We come to understand that life and death are intimately and ultimately connected. For everyone.

Illness comes with a formidable invitation to notice the sacredness of life. It is a wake-up call to life's preciousness. A call to notice the everyday, to be present "here" and "now." To place our lives in perspective to others, to our universe. To accept the place we have in infinity and eternity. To ask the "big" questions and enjoy the "simple" answers. To do this, we must find a rightful place for the suffering. A perspective that allows room for hope. Serious illness is a journey, a hopeful journey, an unknown destination. In illness the dichotomies are vivid. Hope is the space between symptoms and diagnosis, between diagnosis and prognosis. It is the wrestling match between science and compassion, between body and spirit, between

pain and relief. It is the dilemma between fearing to be alone and hungering for privacy.

Hoping is waiting: for test results, for appointments, for the organism to heal and the spirit to rekindle. Hoping is walking the line between tolerating constant probing and invasions, and declaring "no more, not now." The hope for survival is not the only hope; many days, not even the overriding hope. The real hope is not to be "in-valid."

Hoping is knowing that someone is making an effort to help. That family is never far away. That the system cares. That what happens is the best of technology and the best of humanness. Hoping is being attended by people who understand that caring makes a difference. An immeasurable difference.

Hoping is being treated, not as another case of a particular disease, but as a person. By people who understand this could happen to them. It is knowing there are no secrets. Being a partner on the treatment team. Being encouraged to do as much as possible for one's self. Hoping is trying again. Moving against the odds. Knowing everything that can be done is being done. Knowing the caring will go on when the limits of science are reached.

Hoping is denying the statistics. Reaching beyond the traditional. Keeping open the possibility of being the exception. Hoping is listening to the unconscious. Having dreams in the world of sleep and dreams in the world of the conscious. Wondering if there are miracles. Being fascinated with the little miracles: the words that heal, the memories that let us forget.

Hoping is having passion for life. Noticing life. Wanting life. Inching toward life. Being willing to embrace life despite the risks. Hoping is recognizing that death is not the enemy — never living is.

Suffering humbles us; hoping takes us forward. We come to understand that we are among many who are ill. Among many who hurt and fear. And who need. We come to trust the unusual experiences we cannot explain. The experiences for which we have no words. There is a *knowing* that accompanies suffering; a knowing that emerges from deep within us. That speaks from another dimension to life.

With my illness came a "knowing." A "knowing" that my education or my basic goodness does not make me immune. I knew my brother could be ill. I knew others could die. This new knowing has no words. It is a "knowing" that comes from noticing the unexplainable: the dreams, the power of caring, the sense of trust. This knowing is intimately connected with my hope. I recognize that hoping is being able to trust myself. To sense who else is trustworthy. To sense that death is not the worst of stings. To notice that life is available for celebrating. To appreciate the remarkableness in the ordinary. To notice the simple things: the ten-inch scar that brought me new life. The wonderful wiggliness of puppies and how they ignore illness and cuddle. The laughter of a child at blowing bubbles. I know that hope is in the gratitude for today, the mystery of tomorrow.

It's winter. I have the croup again. We're in the car. I think it's the old Chevy with the rounded roof and the side door with all the cigar-lighter marks. My brother Tommy put them there one day when Mom said, "Wait in the car. I'll just be a few minutes." Well, she didn't come back for quite a while. He pushed in the lighter and then used it like a stamp on the side of the door. It looked pretty nifty, so he did it over and over. Making a pattern on the door. Boy, did he get it! That was when the car was brand new.

The wipers are moving back and forth to the sound of my mom's voice. She is saying, real slow, real gently, "It's okay. Breathe slowly. It's okay." The way she says it, I just do it that way. I'm not afraid. I just keep watching her face. If she's afraid, she doesn't show it. I breathe like she tells me. Slowly. Very slowly. No gasping. Just breathing a little bit at a time.

There are two or three men walking in front of the car, shovelling as they go. My dad is one of them. I don't know who is driving the car. The road has a lot of snow drifts, so we are going pretty slowly. Everybody seems real busy. I know everyone is trying to clear the road to get me to the hospital. I know they will.

I like it when Mom reads us a story at night. We're all on Nels and Tom's bed. They sleep together 'cause Tom is diabetic, and he could go into coma when he's sleeping and die. So Nels sleeps with him 'cause if Tom goes into coma, he starts kicking and wakes up Nels. Then Nels can get Mom and Dad. It's scary standing there watching because I don't know what to do. But my mom and dad do. They get the orange juice and the honey and the knife and a washcloth, and they put the wash cloth over the dull knife and try to pry Tom's teeth open and pour in the orange juice and honey. One of them has to hold him down. He doesn't remember anything in the morning. But Nels and I do. That's why Tom and Nels sleep together. 'Cause Tom could die.

The nurse came once and showed us how to put a needle into an orange. And we did it over and over, so if we ever needed to do it for Tom, we could. It's not all bad. If any of us gets hungry on the way home from school, we can stop at the neighbors' and say that Tom is weak, and we all get something to eat. But I wish he didn't have diabetes.

My brothers are settled between the covers, and I am under the extra quilt. Mom asks, "Are you comfy?" Then she starts. I don't care what she reads. Sometimes she reads stories from the *Bible for Kids*. That's okay, but I liked *The Yearling* better. Mostly, I just like her coming up to tuck us in. After she reads to us, she comes with me to my room and tucks me in.

The surgery went wrong. The pneumonia and the infection took their toll. Going back to school is hard. I have missed almost three months, and this is my senior year. I am still in a wheelchair much of the time. I look presentable enough now. That helps. Mr. Marchand thinks I should just stay home until next fall and start again. I know he thinks he is being helpful. I find it a bit discouraging. Mr. Brown dropped the major paper requirement for me. I don't know if I will ever get the hang of permutations and combinations in math. Chemistry is a challenge. Mr. Brock has summarized the whole course for me into forty pages. He says, "Just memorize it. It's your only chance." He works with me after school for a while each afternoon. I tire easily, so we don't concentrate that long. What really helps is that he shares something about himself. He talks to me like a person, not like a teacher. He tells me about lots of things that really aren't chemistry. We have been talking about cryogenics. He has a heart condition, so I think he thinks about life and death, too. I love those talks. And he looks like Burt Lancaster!

Illness, I hate you. I hate you, I hate you for the limitations. I hate the constant need to be energy-efficient. I hate the constant requirement of discipline. Illness, you are a thief. I laugh less. I run less. I risk less. I hate you for making me wonder if others see me as a broken toy. I hate you for the fatigue. I am better at pain than fatigue. Fatigue robs.

This illness is harder, much harder, than ten years ago when the surgery went wrong.

I'm bored. Work, cook, sleep, and deal with my illness. I just don't feel like being adult another hour. The pain is too much. It is like a meat cleaver wedged into a watermelon, like a hot iron pressing a leaf of lettuce.

"Pain, what are you about?"

"I can get you, can't I! I can bring you to tears."

"So, you can bring me to tears. So what?"

"I can make you want to give up."

"You didn't used to, but you can now."

"So I am more powerful than your power of love!"

"I suppose you are — but only in me. Not over all."

"I only have to get individual people to give up."

"You are almost demonic. I thought you were a friend, warning me of physical condition, but you sound almost evil."

"I won't let you know what I really am. You have to figure it out on your own."

"I'm tired of figuring, tired of being positive. Maybe I am just using denial. Maybe I am on a thread, and the thread has vaseline, and I will just slip, no matter how many knots I tie."

"That's it, Baby. Just keep thinking that way."

"I used to be able to banish you."

"Ah! I am winning."

"Today, you probably are. Tomorrow, we do battle again."

I want the camera. I know it doesn't make much sense, but I want the camera. I have saved over three hundred dollars from my graduate research assistant's salary to get it. They are on sale now at the SuperDrug on 17th. All I need is someone to drive me there. I want the camera!

Walt, my racquetball buddy, is reluctant. Not about the camera, but he can see how sick I am. I know it is hurting him to see me trying to even function. Nevertheless, he is there for me. He walks to the pace of my shuffle. He is carrying my purse where I have my chequebook. He senses my anticipation and refrains from saying all the logical but negative things. I am thinking them myself: "Why are you spending three hundred dollars on a camera you can't even carry because you have so much pain? How do you think you are going to take any pictures in your health?"

A small but stronger voice speaks: "Never mind. Buy the camera. Trust me."

My handwriting looks foreign. It is shaky. I assure the clerk, "There is enough money to cover the camera." His look is gentle and unconcerned. I sense he senses the illness. Walt carries the camera and the purse. We shuffle back to the car. I am exhausted and proud. The camera sleeps with me for a week. We begin a long friendship.

It is the morning of the last day of the workshop. The leaders are powerful veteran therapists. I don't have a traditional psychology or medical training, so I am like a sponge. I want to absorb it all. The invitation comes: "We have been asked if we could demonstrate some dream work. Is there anyone who has had a dream and is interested in working on it?"

There is a momentary silence. No one volunteers. Another moment. I glance around and then with deliberateness I offer, "Well, I have had four dreams, but they are all about death."

There is no hesitation on their part. They motion me to stay where I am and begin with, "Simply tell us the dream as if you were right there."

I share two of the dreams briefly but descriptively. I first tell of being invited to a house for dinner. When I arrive, everyone at the table is dead. I begin to tell about the second dream in which a little sheep dog is drawing my attention to the back of the truck I am driving. In it there are a number of dead bodies.

A voice intrudes, "Have you been ill?"

"I think so, but no one in the medical world seems to think so. I have lost thirty-five pounds, and I throw up all the time. And the pain at night is really bad."

Their words to me are, "We need to stop this. Will you meet with us at lunch?" They turn to the group and in an instructional voice state, "This is not a dream of a psychological nature. This woman is physically ill. Is there anyone else who is willing to share a dream?"

At lunch the three of us sit down at a small table away from the group. They fire off questions one after another: "What are you experiencing physically? Who have you seen? How strong is your will to live?" I give them the short version. Their eyes stay directly on me. Their parting words to me are, "Don't let anyone tell you this is in your head. Do whatever you need to do to get well."

I take their directive seriously. If there is to be any hope, I must trust my own deepest self. The self that speaks in dreams.

"How are your bowels?"

"Fine."

"Have they moved today?"

"Oh, God, I hope not. Where would they go?"

"Does your stool float?"

"I don't know. I rarely watch."

The resident taking this fine history informs me that I will never see her again, so I abandon my effort to establish "human" communication and quietly submit to unexplained probes, some of which I suspect are in response to my one-and-only attempt to relate. I had asked, "How did you come to choose internal medicine?"

Her response had not been comforting. As she put unusual pressure on my lower abdomen, she replied: "I couldn't stand obstetrics and gynecology. You'd understand if you spent your whole day investigating intrauterine infections in complaining women. I couldn't stand pediatrics. That was a nightmare. Surgery was boring. It didn't hold my attention."

As I listened, I quietly hoped any surgeon I had would not feel the same way.

She went on: "Surgeons tend to become good technicians. They don't relate to people."

I thought, lady, if you think this is relating, thank God I didn't get a surgical resident to do the admitting medical.

She went on: "Psychiatry, NEVER!"

I resolved not to tell her I was a psychologist.

"Pathology, I like. It's detective work. I'm not much interested in treatment, though."

I softly added, "That's where my interest most lies presently."

It took six weeks to see him. I spoke with him for only minutes before the biopsy. He gave the diagnosis to a nurse on a slip of paper and told her to give it to my mom. I have been in the hospital twelve days now without seeing him again. I have had the parade of interns and residents, but today I am determined to see him. I can't keep the medications down even when I wrap them in bread. They just come up along with other stuff that looks like wet charcoal.

His first words are, "I don't make social calls."

"It's not your friendship I need."

The discussion doesn't improve. It becomes clear: I am the patient; he is the doctor. He will tell me what I need to know and when I need to know it, and I am to do as he orders.

His closing comment is, "I am too busy to be answering all these questions. I work sixty-five hours a week."

Mine is, "Perhaps you could refer me to someone who has time. I am not sure I want to be under the care of someone who is so overextended."

He leaves without comment. His protégé awkwardly follows. The resident's eyes meet mine. He is embarrassed. I, strangely, feel a little stronger.

I have another question. It takes me a minute or two to put on my robe and shuffle out of the ward. Yes, he is still at the desk. His back is toward me. His intern is intently questioning. Neither sees me. I hear the next question: "Why don't you operate?"

I hear the answer: "You don't operate on personalities like Jevne. She'll be sick all her life, and guys like me and you will pay for her welfare."

I say nothing. I don't feel crushed. I consider the source. I feel strong and grounded, but I have no energy for a confrontation. The words inside are, 'You arrogant powermonger. You have known me for less than twenty minutes, half of which I was anesthetized, and you are prepared to judge my character and my whole future! You know nothing about me. If you were once human, you have long since lost that. I may die, but at least I am still human.'

I feel good leaving the hospital. Knowing that we are going to try something. That I am taking the risk of getting out from under the tyranny of arrogance. It's hard to believe that Mom had to contact a lawyer to get my records. The doctor is a little shaken, I think. It seems his determination to have any error go undetected exceeds his confidence. He knows we are going to Mayo. He knows it is another physician who has recommended it. When Mom spoke to me about going, she had asked, "How will you get there?" I had whispered, "I have reserve." She had shaken her head, caught between two risks. Which was the greater? Staying here with the known or going again into the unknown? I was clear: We go. Arrangements have been made to leave for Rochester tomorrow. We stay at the farm tonight.

It is good to be back home — the home with the good smells, the bedroom with the special things of my childhood, the kitchen table with the view of the yard. It feels right to stay here overnight before we leave. I am a bit shaky but okay.

I am surprised to see the minister sitting at the table. I lean against the planter and kid him, saying, "Aren't you here a little early?" He obviously isn't prepared for how I look. His tears mix with laughter.

The next morning we have to get to the airport. It is an effort to mount the step into my brother's van, but it means I can lie down on the way. Oh, there's Dad and his camera. Everyone gathers around the wheelchair, niece and nephew included. Never mind, with Dad taking the picture, the heads will be cut off anyway. I smile inside. The farewell photo is almost amusing.

I decide I want to sit in the seat in the front. It will recline. Before I lower it, I look out at my dad and I wonder, 'Will I ever see my dad again.' There is a lump in my throat.

I wish my brother's van wasn't black.

I am eighty-eight pounds. I look like a Biafran commercial for relief funds. There are tubes. Tubes out of everywhere. Places I didn't know you can put tubes, and tubes that they had to cut holes for. And the resuscitator, or whatever it is called, is doing my breathing for me. It is only the pillows that give me form. Like a huge neonatal case, lying on cotton batting.

I don't know how it happened. I have fallen off my pillows. It strikes me as funny. I don't even try to get untangled. There is no strength. And there seems to be no need. I'm not going anywhere. There is just a silly little giggle. And it hurts! 'Slipped off my pillows. Slipped off my pillows.' I smile. A huge grin on the inside, 'What is the point of having a Ph.D. when I can't even get back on my pillows? Now that's a cosmic joke.'

It is one of those moments I had read about in philosophy class. One of those *existential* moments. Doesn't being well-educated give me an immunity to being ill? Or maybe even to dying? I giggle again. And it hurts.

For days we live with the uncertainty. The day comes to "test the system." One of the Pink Ladies comes right on time. Into the wheelchair, slowly. Down to X-ray. Past the room where I had had the sigmodoscopy. Where I had been lined up with a dozen others for an unsavory test. Everyone else in the line had been at least seventy years old. I had ignored what their eyes said as they calculated my age.

I am determined to show the technicians how much strength I have. I stand for the occasion. Of course, I have to. But I will do it without help. I will do it myself. I drink the yellow stuff. I expected it to be white like the barium. But it is yellow. Maybe it will make me glow. I can't see. The room is dark.

Two of the surgical residents are there. They make remarks about how good they are getting at stitching. How I won't have much of a scar. With an obvious weakness in my voice, I complement them: "I am impressed at how you can do a bypass with such a little scar. I am amazed that you can work in such a little area."

Each looks at the other. One smirks. The tallest offers, "What makes you think we worked inside?"

I am not quite sure what he means. I decide I don't want to know.

The technician is nodding her head. Our attention returns to the task at hand. The openness in her face and her obvious gentle smile draws everyone's attention. The residents are silent. They say nothing, but it's like they are cheering. They are obviously pleased. Partly for them. Partly for me. What we had hoped for is happening.

I am being discharged today. We have been asked to stay in Rochester for a couple more days before returning to Canada. Just precautionary. If everything remains stable, we will be home soon. My mom tells me Jeannie is leaving today, too. Jeannie is twenty three. I am twenty nine. Her mother is at her side, as mine is at mine. Mothers of hope have a way of being there in uncertainty. I have never met Jeannie, but my mom reports daily on her progress. Our moms talk each day. They are both here with what is most precious to them. They are both scared. They are both hoping. Jeannie is doing quite well, too.

Mom is putting my nighties and the cards into my overnight case. Dr. Van Heerdan and his troop are here, early as usual. They all have that "clean cut" look, like their mothers scrubbed them. Dr. Van Heerdan sits close to my shoulder. Like he did the first day I met him. He asked no questions. He only said quietly, "You are so thin. We need to do something about that." Now our time together is over. I am going home.

All I can say is, "Thank you." I sense uncertainty in his voice. His eyes meet mine as he says, "We haven't given you a miracle. We may have given you an aspirin for a brain tumor. But you will be able to eat. We hope we have given you a good year. Go home and live with a good deal of common sense. And what will be will be."

I have no words. Only the thought, 'How do I thank someone for my life?'

The connections back to Canada are iffy at best. We have been trying for several days to get a flight through to Edmonton. With the flood in Rochester and the airline strike, getting home isn't easy. Finally, there is the option of being confirmed to Winnipeg and going stand-by from there. Mom is reluctant. I am convinced we will get on. I promise, "We'll be okay." Fine for me to say. It's Mom who will have to handle everything.

We go.

There is a layover in Minneapolis. It's lunch time. The wheelchair fits nicely under the table in the restaurant. We can see the planes coming and going. It seems so busy. How do they all land and take off and never hit each other? It's a miracle there isn't a collision a day. The waitress returns to see if we need anything. She is right out of the 1950s. Her hair is bleached and back-combed. Her apron starched. Her make-up is this side of gaudy. She is as busy as the runways. Mom responds "No, we are fine." And smiles as she watches me sip my soup.

The waitress asks, "Are you coming or going?" The way she looks at me leaves no doubt she is referring to coming or going to Mayo.

We say in unison, "We're going home."

With the clatter of dishes in the background, she leans forward, puts her hand on my mom's shoulder, and says, "You got your miracle. Isn't that wonderful?"

There is no doubt she knows something only moms know. Something special. The tears well up. My mom's eyes meet hers, "Yes, it is." Mom pauses. Then she adds, with a giggle, "So why am I crying in my soup?"

Even in the darkness I know something is wrong. "What is it, Allen?"

"I have pain."

"Severe?"

"It's not going away. I've tried nitro twice. We better head for emergency."

"Should I call 9-1-1?"

"I think we can make it on our own this time."

"Are you sure?"

"Yeah."

He pulls on his jeans with some effort. Somehow I am fully dressed without even knowing how. His left hand is using my right forearm for support. We're halfway across the room. The motion beside me stops. Allen shakes his head. And slumps.

"Hang on, Hon."

The phone is only feet away. The 9-1-1 call is quick. They keep me on the line while they dispatch the ambulance.

"Yes, there is a pulse. It's steady. Yes, I know how to take it."

It is only minutes before they are here. Five paramedics arrive. They all seem to be doing something. One seems unquestionably in charge.

"Hello, Mr. Eng. We've met before. We'll have you comfortable in a few minutes. Can you answer a few questions for me?"

I find myself answering other questions: "Do you know what medication he is on? When did this start?"

I am in control until I am back in bed, hours later. Allen is in intensive care but stable. I am exhausted. My eyes won't close. The bed seems too big. The sobbing begins.

Being back in the hospital myself feels like an invitation to fear again. Being back in pain torments more than my body. I have to struggle not to feel like a failure, not to feel like I could have prevented whatever is wrong and yet unnamed, but obviously serious. Most likely it is the same illness that challenged me years ago. I know that I have often near-exhausted the energy, the energy that I had found in the journey back to health. How many times in the last decade have I heard myself say, "I don't know if I could fight it twice." Now it looks like I will have to decide.

I lie back on the stiff foam pillow that is really an emergency ward pillow. The ward pillows are supposed to be softer. This one could serve as a hardball base. I have to get ahold of myself. I have to reach deep. I have been in the hospital only one day. After fourteen years, they are using the word "reoccurrence." I can't know at this moment that in five days they will say, "Gee, we were wrong." For now, fear is my unwelcome intruder.

Imagery. Imagery. Transform the images. The wall at the foot of my bed is bare. At least it doesn't have a haunting crucifix that stares at every agnostic at a vulnerable time. Images dance on the wall. Skeletons, hideously dancing, as if awaiting a tribal feast. They are feasting on my foolishness. My foolish belief that I can lick this if I am just careful, if I just do things right. I need an image of health, not illness. I need to act on what can be, not what is at this moment. I need to stop lying here catastrophizing. To stop allowing the images to haunt me. What will be will be. What can I do to intentionally focus on possible health?

I call Allen.

"Hon, will you bring me my sweatsuit and my running shoes? I need them."

"Sure. But what for?"

"I need out of this gown. I need to redefine myself. I choose not to be a patient."

The Voice of the "other"

A S HEALTH CAREGIVERS, WE THINK OF THE PATIENT as the "other." We have an illusion they are unlike us. That they are "other" than us. We assume we are knowledgeable about their bodies and their feelings and their souls. If we are open, these others whom we call "patients" become our teachers. Those who have walked the walk are the mentors of hope. We learn from them. We learn the lessons of hope in the voices that are saying:

> Hear us. Speak to us, not about us. Understand that we have parts of our lives that you do not know. Touch us. Know that we are more than the bodies you treat. Like you, we have spouses and friends and work. Keep to yourself your judgments about who we are; about who you would be under the same circumstances. Understand that we are afraid and courageous. That we want and don't want to be informed. That we are indebted to you and angry that we need your help. Know that we need you to believe that there is some kind of hope. If you cannot help our physical conditions, help us hope for something within our control. Understand that your words and your attitude can be lethal to our hope.

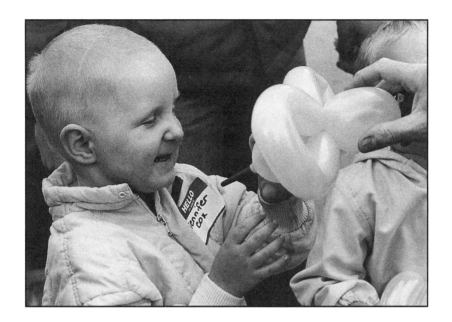

In the world of suffering, those of us called "caregivers" grapple to find a rightful place for hope in our "professional" frameworks. We wrestle with roles and policies and procedures as they come in conflict with our sense of what is truly needed. We search for our own unique coordinates between expert and person, bureaucracy and immediacy, the respectful and the invasive. Between knowing and guessing. We struggle to find a way of being that is truly hopeful. There is a temptation to stay protected from another person's uniqueness. To turn away from the lessons they offer.

Whether the "other" is young or old, religious or agnostic, of our culture or of those foreign, they teach us what it means to heal. What it means to hope. They don't tell us; they show us. The young mother who vows to walk her son to his first day of school. The little fellow who pushes his intravenous with one hand and cradles his kidney basin in another, as he searches the hallway for someone to fix the broken truck he holds securely under his arm. The young dad who struggles with nausea on a day pass during chemotherapy to see his son run the 880. They show us how meaning is woven in to the fabric of their hopes. And we begin to learn.

We begin to be able to show that we, too, hope. The volunteer stays the night to soften the aloneness. The doctor drops by on a Saturday morning. We learn how important the little things are: the bedside table left within reach, the late night rendezvous, the card that says what we couldn't. We are appreciative when someone is grateful for what we do. And we grow in understanding of what it means to care and to contribute to hope.

The meaning of hope begins to be conscious. We begin to see the components: time, authenticity, advocacy, risk. Each taught by an experience. Some understandings take many lessons. Others are learned in a moment, forever imprinted. We admit the gap between our intent to help and the limits of our knowledge. Sometimes we want out, but we stay and are seduced to more lessons.

We begin to be intentional about hope. We begin to be more present. When the need is there, not later − now. We begin to listen without judgment. To accept that there are multiple realities. We struggle to accept each patient's unique reality, to honor their values. To understand this is ultimately their life. That we are, at most, an invited guest; at worst, an interloper who shatters hope. We are the constant observers to the live theater of courage and strength in the drama of hope for which there are no lines. It is all impromptu. We learn that life is not a dress rehearsal.

For me, the lessons began the first day at the clinic in a cancer hospital: Authenticity is to be cherished. Simplicity, appreciated. Caring counts. Distance is generally not welcome and not necessary. Humor has its place. Commitment is powerful. Risking is rewarded. Listening is an art. Words are powerful. Community is stronger than isolation. Differences can happen. When the depths of the human spirit have been reached, we can go deeper. Children are amazing. Pain and suffering are not synonymous. We know so little. Mistakes do happen. Miracles do occur. Good-byes are hard. Hoping is knowing the uncertainty will never stop. Nor will the lessons. Nor will the gifts.

It is my first day in the clinic. There has been no orientation. It's sink or swim. This woman is my first client. I know from the chart that she is in her early forties. The room is small. A kind of hospital blue. No pictures. Two doors: one for the treatment team, one for the patient. It's like they enter from two different worlds. The stirrups on the treatment table seem out of place. The woman I am facing is not facing me. She has turned the chair to the cement block wall. She utters, "I told the doctor, I don't want to talk to you."

There is no textbook solution to this. She repeats the words without altering her position. I risk saying, "I think I know some of what you are feeling."

Her quick and cutting response comes back, "No, you don't."

I am aware that I am hesitant to share my own experience. I am also aware that nothing short of doing so is going to give me the right to stay in this room. "I am going to talk for a minute or two and if, at the end, you still believe that, I will respect your wishes and leave. Is it anything like this? You wish you'd never have to come here again, and yet you are afraid you might be told you don't have to come any more because there is nothing more they can do. You want to be left alone, yet you are afraid everyone will leave. You want to scream at everything, yet you know there is no one to blame. You want to be brave, and you are terrified. You can't look at your children without fighting the lump in your throat. You want to be held, yet you want to be composed." More words flow out in a voice that doesn't sound like mine. I stop.

She holds the sides of her chair and, without rising, she turns to face me. "You do know some of what I feel. How do you know?"

"I have been at least part way there."

"I think you have."

"I don't know if I can help. I can only promise I will journey with you."

"A toque?"

"Yes, a toque. A knitted toque. The kind of hat that looks like a big loose sock pulled over your head. The kind you wear for skiing. And he pulls it further down each day. We have found a translator. Maybe she can help you figure out what is really happening."

We agree I will meet the translator at the nursing station at 11:00 a.m.

Sure enough, he is wearing a toque. I have no idea whether he is mad, bad, sad, or bonkers. I just see an elderly man who looks little in his bed. If I hadn't looked at his chart, I couldn't have guessed his age. His toque covers his hair line. His face is weathered and strong. His intravenous pole seems to hold him hostage. I am there to assess his depression, but he looks more distraught than depressed.

During the first few minutes, it is obvious that the translator is connecting with him. About what, I don't know. I can imagine it is about his homeland. It could as easily have been about the absurdity of hospitals. He speaks with animation to the woman who is his link with our world.

The translator conveys, "He wants his daughter to come from overseas. He thinks he is dying. Can you help him contact her?"

"What makes him think he is dying?"

They speak intently. There is no lightness now as in the first few minutes.

"He says he can tell from all the pain in his abdomen."

"What does he think is causing the pain?"

The interaction is brief. Only two words.

"The cancer."

"Can you tell him that the pain is temporary and is from the treatment he is getting?" I am confident in saying that because his case was discussed at rounds this morning.

She turns and relays the information. Mr. S. shakes his head in disbelief. He looks as me suspiciously as he talks.

"He says he is getting no treatment and that his doctor doesn't even come to see him. That we are very rude to an old and dying man."

For a second or two I am puzzled. Can it be?

"Ask him if he goes downstairs each day on a stretcher."

A pause. "Yes, he does."

"What does he think happens down there?"

His eyebrows raise and lower as he speaks.

"They leave him in a dark room — alone. And then just take him back to his bed. They do nothing!"

It is sinking in. This man has no understanding of radiation.

"Ask him if his doctor has explained through a translator what is going on in that dark room."

"He says he has never seen a doctor."

I am momentarily puzzled again. I know who his doctor is. "Will you describe Dr. M. to him and ask if she doesn't see him, at least on occasion?"

He seems to dismiss the question. His arm gestures the dismissal.

"He says women are not doctors."

"Thank you. I may need you again in a while."

"I will stay and talk with him for a few minutes."

We confer. We need a male intern to explain the radiation treatments and to drop by regularly. In two days Mr. S. is boldly pushing his intravenous up and down the hallways, striding as if in training for a whole new way of life.

I have been warned. This will be a difficult one. This is a "multi-problem" family. The referring physician knows how unlikely it is that we will be able to do what a multiple of social services have been unable to do. This is one of those times when I wish my role was to write a report about what is wrong rather than to make a difference. 'Never mind,' I tell myself. 'Get up there. Either get started or get rejected.' I am intrigued by this family. In some ways, meeting with them will be either a win or a draw for me. At best, I can help. At worst, I will be as inadequate as those before me.

The room is across the hall from the nursing station. Being close like that usually means the patient needs greater care. Lloyd is in the bed beside the window. He is a big man. He hardly fits in the bed. He is already slightly jaundiced. Joyce, his wife, is a solid woman. She has an open face, nothing wimpy looking about her. Her eyes follow me in. A stalky lad on the window sill has his face buried in a comic book. From him there is only a quick glance.

"Good morning. I am Ronna Jevne." I let my name tag signal my credentials. I sense it is not the time to extend my hand for the shake that binds.

With a quickness in her voice, Joyce states, "I know you."

I reply with, "I'm sorry, I don't recognize you."

"No, I wouldn't think that you would. I remember you because you and, I assume, your husband and your mother had dinner in the restaurant where I was a waitress. You drink hot water and lemon."

"Yes, I do."

"I remember how kind all of you were and how you all laughed so much. What do you do here?"

"I talk with families who are having a challenging time."

"Well, that's us. We can use all the help we can get."

"Dr. Jevne, you're interested in long-term survivors. There's a woman down here you might want to meet."

"Sure, I'll be down in a few minutes."

The technician motions me into the room off the waiting area. Up goes the film. The light behind shows what even I recognize as a backbone. "Take a look at this. You would wonder how she can even walk. She's had cancer twenty-six years. She comes every year for her checkup."

I look intently at what looks like an X-ray. "She's not having any problems. You just want me to meet her?"

"Yeah, she's interesting."

Emily is seventy-five if she is a day. A little wiry body with a stoop that is slight but noticeable. Her cane is beside her. It's nothing fancy. Just plain and wooden. She rises when the technician says, "Emily, this is Dr. Jevne. She is interested in meeting you."

"Is there something wrong?"

"No, not at all. I just like meeting people who have done so well."

"My daughter is picking me up. Are you going to see me to the door?"

"I would love to."

She takes my forearm. The cane seems to be more for balance than anything. She chatters as we near the escalator.

"I have been coming here for twenty-six years."

She stops while we ride the moving stairs. Not a word. Not a sideways glance as we ride to the foyer. She steps off. Continues to look straight ahead.

"Your mind has a lot to do with it, you know. But it's not easy. This arthritis is getting worse every year. Oh, there's my daughter."

I escort her out the door to the waiting car. It is parked just under the sign, *Cancer Institute*. I wonder at the marvel of selective perception. I think how funny it would be if we changed the sign to *Arthritis Institute*.

Herb is a man who has always been in charge of his family. His wife doesn't drive, he makes the decisions, and he loves her dearly. The feelings are mutual. He's a golfer. He has loved his retirement. There is plenty of time for his golf.

He is in a four-bed unit in the far bed by the window. It is a beautiful July morning. I have no agenda in dropping by. Just thought I would see how things are going. I approach quietly.

"If you're going to say something positive, you can leave right now."

I ask, "Want to tell me more?"

"A nurse comes in, throws open the blinds, and says, 'What a wonderful, beautiful day.' Then two minutes later another one comes in and does the same thing."

"And you didn't want to hear that."

"Would you, if someone had just told you would never walk again?"

"Herb, I'm sorry. That must be very hard."

We talk for a while. More accurately, I listen, he talks. What I hear helps me understand how everything in his life, his work, his play, everything has involved his legs. He is thinking about giving up. I sense it is more than a moment of despair. It is not for me to decide or even to coach. But I can question.

"It seems that you know who you were with legs. Have you any interest in finding out who you are without legs?"

"I don't know. Maybe. I'm not sure."

"It wouldn't be easy, but it might be important."

Two days pass before we talk again. This time his wife, Trudi, is at the bedside. I haven't more than set my clipboard down when he announces, "My wife has agreed to take driving lessons."

A moment of unspoken respect passes between him and me.

Ruby is a strong-willed woman who has obviously managed considerable adversity in her life. Now in her time of need she feels that her children are not doing enough. The same with the neighbors. She rants and raves and judges them in my presence. Her anger is recorded in my new rug. Each time, she jams her cane into it for emphasis. My new dusty rose rug! My new dusty rose rug that the volunteers paid for. Its first marks. I try not to look wounded. She concludes with questions to me: "Why do they ignore me? Why can't they care more?"

I am honestly intimidated by her and say so: "Maybe because they feel what I am feeling. I feel like there is nothing I could say or do that would ever be enough. I don't know if that is true. That's just the way I feel. You come across so strong and so judgmental."

I add, "Perhaps they don't see the hurt below your anger."

In a strong Germanic accent, she retorts, "You think so?"

"Maybe. I don't know."

- - - - - -

To my surprise she is back in a week. She has a broad, warm smile. She by-passes the preliminaries and gets to the point: "Why didn't anyone tell me I was a beetch? I haf' been a beetch. I didn't even know. I was just so hurt. I didn't even know. I talked to my boys, and it will be better now. Why didn't anyone else tell me? Things can be different now that I know."

It is wonderful to escape the winter. To sit for hours in silence with Allen in our little private room. On the train everything is so compact, but it's fun. There are no interruptions. No traffic to concern us. No telephone calls! Just book after book to inhale. The mountains never lose their majesty. Mile after mile of mountains call me back to perspective. Back to how little I am. Back to an awareness that I am fragile. It's a quiet feeling. Endlessly staring out the window returns me to a place where I understand the silliness of the human ego.

I am hungry. I have sailor's legs as we move down the dining car. There is a stout older woman, maybe sixty, walking toward us. I know her. No, it can't be. Then the voice confirms it: "Dr. Jevne." She is still ten feet away.

"Ruby?"

"Ya. You think I was dead?" Her voice seems to boom.

"It's good to see you." I'm not sure if my voice betrays me. Indeed, I would have assumed she was dead. It must be seven years since she was diagnosed.

"You remember me!"

"Sure, I remember you." How could I forget her? Her anger is still recorded in my rug.

Her voice booms over the background noise of the train: "The doctor, he says I am a miracle."

She turns to Allen and in her German way asks me, "This your man?"

"Yes."

She turns to him and looks him directly in his eyes. No small feat for someone pushing five feet. She had lost inches with the bone cancer.

"Your wife, she's a good woman. She give me back my hope."

There was that word again.

Jim thinks of himself as a high-powered businessman. And he is. But his pain has stolen his public profile; it has sentenced him to a life totally foreign to him. The limits it has placed on him are nearly intolerable. I see him after hours so no one will know he is coming to the "banana farm." He is still walking across the room when he starts questioning me. He is not yet seated before he challenges: "Why didn't you tell me?"

"Tell you what?"

"Tell me that it's not the pain that will kill me. It's the suffering. It's the not-workin'. The not-golfin'. The not-being-able to make a contribution to my community. That's what's killin' me.

"They had already told me there wasn't any more they could do. When I asked you the same thing I asked them — 'What are my options?' — you said, 'Sure you have options.' I naively asked, 'Well, what are they?' And you answered, 'You could die!'

"Well, that set me back. It set me back in the car all the way home. I was mad at you all week. But you're right. Up until now I thought the docs were goin' to do everything for me. Now I know I gotta do part of this. I gotta build a wall between hope and hopeless. And I better get doin' it right now."

The waiting, the waiting, the waiting. It's nearly six. Most of the staff have gone home. I am going down the outpatient department hallway. I am on my way home. Most of the lights are out. There are no windows in Area D. Sitting there is Dot, my mother's friend. She has advanced breast cancer. She looks like an insignificant doll in an oversized chair. She is the mother of four. Four whom she will not see reach teenagehood. Her shoulders are rounded. Her head drooping some from the fatigue.

"Dot, what are you doing here?"

"I am waiting for the doctor."

The tension in her voice betrays her. She fights back a tear.

"Are you in pain?"

"No. I guess I am just upset. I have been waiting for three hours. A few minutes ago I knocked on the door of the treatment room. The nurse answered, so I asked her, 'When will I be seen? I'm so tired.' She just said, 'We are all tired,' and closed the door. Ronna, I can't handle much more."

I have no words. I just sit down to wait with her. I am tired, too. This damn disease has a way of getting us all tired.

Her eyes don't meet mine, but then that isn't uncommon for aboriginal Canadians. I know she usually sees Mark.

"No, Mark won't be in at all today."

"Well, I wanted ta' see him, and I'm goin' back up north today."

"I have time, if you think I could help."

"Well, ya, okay."

We step into the small office. There is hardly room to turn around. The only advantage to this pencil box office is that it forces a certain proximity.

She looks earnestly at me: "Well, it's the guilt." The pause seems to tell me it is my turn.

"Can you tell me more about the guilt?"

"Well, I am doin' real good. The lumps are goin' down, and I feel real good except for when I come here. I hate comin' here. When I come here, I feel like I am sick. Back home, I never do. So, I am gettin' well. The doctor is real proud."

"Can you help me understand what getting well has to do with your guilt?"

"Well, ya see, they give me these here pills that I am supposed to take. But I don't. I go to our own medicine man. I take what he gives me. I just come here because I like to get the pictures that tell me if I am gettin' better. But it bothers me that I don't tell the doctors that I don't take their medicine."

"I see." A little smirk crosses my face. A little smirk crosses her face. Her dark eyes snap with a flash of mischief. I lean forward and whisper, "I won't tell if you don't."

"You think it's okay then? 'Cause I don't want to tell them, but I don't want to stop comin' for the pictures." She adds, "I am Catholic, you know. I will tell the priest but that's all. Thanks a lot. I feel better now."

Only five minutes have passed since we met. I smile and I am thinking about the science of "controlled studies." Her success will be chalked up as a "win" for science.

I sometimes come to the hospital early in order to see nurses who are coming off shift at 7:00 a.m. I don't mind. It's quiet. Actually, kind of peaceful. It is as if the suffering sleeps. Today, though, I have resolved myself to action. Today I will resign. I am fed up with being treated like a second-class citizen in the helping world. I am tired of the nonsense about whether patients can talk to us. About whether physicians own people. I am tired of patriarchy cloaked in a dozen vestments. I don't need this. Maybe none of it is intentional, but I'm tired of it. There are other options. I am tired of shaking a hand and knowing that, in eight out of ten cases, the way I will close the file is with confirmation on the deceased list. I can't handle the chronic suffering. Someone is always dying. Someone else is in the bed an hour later. I don't even mind the dying. Ultimately death is not in our control. What is within our control, but we are neglecting to notice, is the multiplicity of insensitivities. The waiting time. The hurt from errors of omission. The hurt from errors of commission. Mostly in communication. Occasionally in caring. I have had enough. We would never leave people bleeding in the hallway; they would get immediate attention. Yet when they are emotionally in pain, we not only leave them bleeding but there is also an effort to deny them access to pain relief.

I am getting out. There, it's written. It's brief and to the point. It begins, "This is to inform you of my resignation as Senior Psychologist effective one month from this date."

7:00 p.m. that night.

My resignation is still sitting here. Tomorrow, then. I am too tired to even think about it tonight. What if I don't leave? All the reasons I am using for leaving are why I should stay. They are why Alice stays. They are why Rhea stays. Alice and Rhea think they can make a difference. And they do. I'm not even sure what difference I am supposed to make. Psychology has been here as a discipline for eighteen months, and we are just moving case by case. So what difference do I think is really important?

It is late, and yet my pen cannot be silenced. The writing begins:

I have a dream – a vision of how caring could be. Of how being ill wouldn't mean fear and loneliness, wouldn't mean long days of anxiety. That it could mean coming to an institution that cared. Where a whole institution of caring people understood that nothing is as therapeutic as recognizing the emotional pain, not just the physical pain . . .

I have a vision that doctors could talk compassionately. That families could talk openly. That patients could talk freely. That death could be something to be faced, not feared . . .

I have a vision that caregivers would touch patients, gently, caringly – and not only physically. That all would recognize that with every touch, every smile, every word, we enter a temple. A temple so sacred, so impressionable, so beautiful that every fingerprint leaves its mark . . .

I have a vision that caregivers would share a strength – a strength that comes only from a common purpose, that comes from belonging to a community of people who believe that caring makes a difference, that custodians matter as much as physicians, that volunteers have a place beside nurses, that letters and titles matter less than kindness . . .

That line-ups are no more. That people are cared for before paper. That voices convey caring before directions. That waiting rooms reflect hope rather than convenience. That death means knowing a lot of people care. That there would be no aloneness. That tears could give way to laughter and anger to tenderness. That joy could surface in our sadness . . .

An hour late my pen comes to a rest. There is a new hope and a new commitment.

Phillip's mom is probably going to die today. No one has told him directly yet. The nursing staff has asked me to talk with the dad. I ask him if the children understand the gravity of the situation.

"I'm not sure. I haven't said anything to Phillip. I want him to know, but I just can't tell him."

"Would you like some help telling him?"

"Yes."

The office is small. Phillip sits on the edge of the chair. Even then, he can't touch the floor. His eyes are deep and peaceful. I look at dad who looks to me to lead. "Phillip, do you know how sick your mom is?"

He leans forward. Looks straight at his dad. He speaks calmly and very audibly. "Dad, she's really sick." His hand touches his dad's knee. "She's probably going to die. Maybe today, I think." He is searching to know if his dad is okay with the information. His dad's hand goes over Phillip's on the knee. They both look to me. I feel a lump forming at the back of my throat.

"Phillip, do you have anything you would like to tell your mom if this is the last day she's alive?"

"Yes." The voice is no less sure, just somewhat quieter.

"Would you like anyone to come with you?"

His little head nods a definite yes as his eyes meet mine. He intuitively knows that, with the tension between his mom and dad, this is not the moment for dad to be at mom's bedside.

We walk in silence down the hall. Without ceremony, Phillip signals he wishes to go into the room by himself. He moves the bedside stool so he can get near her. He glances back at me. I nod. He turns to his mom. Her body is still, but her head moves in his direction. He says, simply, "Mom, I love you." Mom's hand reaches for his. In what may have been moments or minutes, he steps down. He puts the stool away and comes to the door where his dad and I are waiting. He looks up and asks his dad, "Don't you think my sisters should know, too? Should I tell them?"

Dad's eyes fill. "We'll go home and both tell them. Okay?"

"Okay."

The voice on the pager says, "Dr. Jevne, there's an Andy who says he has permission to call you any time."

That's true. I have an agreement with Andy that he can call any time, that he can ask anything he wants, and I will try to answer it honestly. I only met Andy yesterday. He'd been throwing rocks where he shouldn't have been throwing rocks. He's been responsible for injuring several youngsters in hockey. His anger is coming out all over. He's a husky kid. A husky kid whose dad is dying. Yesterday his dad was sick, but home. Today he is in intensive care.

"Yes, Andy."

"Could you help me cheer up my dad?"

"I'm not sure your dad feels much like being cheered up, Andy. Would it be okay for your dad just to feel whatever he's feeling for a little while?"

"I guess."

"Do you feel responsible for making him feel better?"

"Sort of."

We talk on about how his dad feels pretty punk and how it might help if he just holds his dad's hand.

- - - - - -

"Dr. Jevne, it's Andy again."

"Thanks. Put him through."

"Do you think that my dad knows that I know?"

We both understood Andy's talking about knowing that his father is dying. We talk about how he might find out what his dad knows.

- - - - - -

"Dr. Jevne, it's Andy again."

"Yes, Andy."

"Well, I did it. I went in and I held his hand and I asked him, 'Dad, do you know that I know?' He looked at me and he smiled. He said, 'No, I didn't, Andy, but I am glad that you do.' It works, Dr. Jevne, it really works. This talking stuff really works."

"Why didn't you call me?"

"It was your day off. We didn't want to bother you."

"Please, when a patient asks for me, you have my permission to bother me."

It had taken me months to develop a trusting relationship with Laura. She was profoundly private. She had told no one about her cancer — not a single person, including her mother, from whom she was estranged, even though they lived in the same city. I suspect, of those on staff, only I and her compassionate physician knew about the suicide of a loved one, the murder of a lover.

When we first talked, it was only about her horse. About whether she should put him down before she died. Because he was a very special horse with special needs, and it was likely no one would be able to take appropriate care of him. She spoke of the hours she spent grooming, despite the fact she could no longer ride. She savored the memories of training him. How she wanted to harness, not break his spirit. She would not put him down. Yet he would be too much trouble for someone else. And what if he were ever mistreated?

The conversations shifted. Illness was always off-limits. But the questions began: "Do you think there is anyone who really could love him? Who would take the time to groom him? Exercise him? Treasure him? Who wouldn't try to change him?" The day came when she decided he would live. It was not long before she was admitted to hospital. She was only in a couple of days before she died. And she was afraid. And she was repeatedly asking for me. And I never came. I never came. How could someone else decide I wouldn't want to be bothered on my day off? I know they were trying to protect me. To give me some space. How could they know the journey we had been on? How could they know the depth of the connection? I need to forgive myself. I need to forgive them. She would have forgiven me.

It is hard sitting here in rounds knowing what I know. I have mixed feelings about rounds. Each week we meet around this boardroom table to discuss "cases." We review over sixty patients in an hour. For the most part, it's no more than a sharing of information.

There is a cacophony of observations. They are talking about Doris.

"There doesn't seem to be any psychosocial support."

"No one ever visits her."

"They are farmers, aren't they?"

"Yeah, she milks cows before most of us get up."

"It's a long ways to drive in. Maybe it's just too far to drive."

"I don't think so. I met her husband once. He is really gruff."

Doris is a woman in her mid-forties. She has children ranging in age from three years old to the early twenties. She and I have had many long talks about her sixteen-year-old. They are a farm family as traditional as one could imagine. Everything is geared to the farm. There is nothing as important as the cows. Children are additional farm labour.

Doris' disease is not kind. Time and time again, she is admitted to the hospital to do what little can be done. She lets me know when she's admitted. Her sharing is unsophisticated and uncensored. She trusts the contract of confidentiality. She has written me her first poem. I know the pain that separates her from her husband. I know how they have shared in creating that distance. I know how Doris is reconciling that with herself and with her God.

All I can say in rounds is, "There are circumstances here that are not generally known. I'm sorry I can't say more. All I can do is ask you to believe and not judge."

There can be no betrayal of Doris' trust. I know everyone who attends rounds has or has had a Doris in their life. We share the struggle for balance between being respectful of privacy and being a team player.

It is 3:30 in the morning. It's a cold Canadian winter night. The street lights guide me along deserted streets. I know my way. I know it well. I have been there many times in the last days. Being in jeans and sneakers somehow adds to the feeling that I am going as a friend. There are no specialists in death. Just friends.

Grace has been moved to the intensive care unit at the University Hospital. It is what she didn't want to happen. She wanted to stay at our hospital. She didn't want the technology. She had said, "When it's time, I want it simple." That was in the talk we had about her "dream." The dream where she went down the tunnel. At least she thinks it was a dream. She started down the tunnel toward the light and then decided she wasn't ready. Now the time has come, and technology is interfering.

The boys are all here. David, who had called me, rises from the green leather straight-back couch that looks like a thrift store contribution to patient care. He is the least handsome of the three boys. That makes him only very handsome. A broad gentle smile, kind eyes. A reasonable amount of confidence for his twenty-two years. Bart, athletic, solid, more aloof, is sitting on the rug just outside the ICU door a few feet away. John, with whom I have spoken most often, gives me a brief and intense hug and says, "Thanks for coming. There isn't really anything you can do."

There isn't much any of us can do, except be together. Each of them looks at me as if I know what to do. They look to me like I think our sheepdog, Meg, looks at me: eager to serve, she circles, waiting for cues as to her purpose. I love these boys. I know the love Grace has for them. I have no words. Just a sense of my jaw clenching. Then consciously softening my eyes. I lower myself onto the floor with Bart. John takes his place beside me. My hand gives his knee a firm squeeze. His arm gives me a big brother hug. He smiles and asks, "What's a nice girl like you doing out at an hour like this?"

We all burst into laughter. The laughter betrays our tension but makes public our fullness at being together. It is a good feeling.

Janet is thirty-one. Eight-by-ten pictures of her two beautiful youngsters are usually on her bedside table. When I come in, she has them clutched to her chest. She is rocking back and forth. There are no words for a moment or two. Her eyes convey a deep, deep something for which there is no word. There is anxiety, but that doesn't cover it. There is something more — or is it less? There is a hollowness, somehow. As if she has seen where few of have glimpsed. She has seen the abyss into which she feels she is being cast while we stand far back from the edge. I know there are complications of the disease that exacerbate the anxiety. We know each other well, and my presence seems to be calming. The most I can do now is to journey with her.

The nurse beckons me as I leave.

"Do you know there has been a psychiatric consult on her? A resident was over this morning. I don't think he has ever seen an advanced cancer patient. She is to be moved to the psych ward." The nurse and I both know that means new faces, new routines, new pressures, let alone the drain of being transported there. All that plus the stigma.

"Why?"

"The resident says she isn't *adjusting* to her dying. Can't you do something? She probably has only a few days to live."

"Are you willing to help?"

"You bet."

Somehow we both know Janet needs an advocate. The move must not happen. And it doesn't.

Pat is a volunteer at the hospital who decided to model for her friends the importance of mammography. It turns out she had cancer. It is in its later stages now. She was chunky; now she is a wisp. She was short; now she is shorter. The sparkle in her eyes isn't gone, though. And she still has her devilish sense of humor.

For weeks she has been looking forward to attending the dedication of an old school as a heritage building. The Governor General, the Queen's representative, is scheduled to be there. Pat is staunch royalist, allegiant to the Queen and outspoken about it. She was to have had a front row seat in her wheelchair at the dedication. Two days before the event, she was admitted to hospital.

Pat is very disappointed. She will be unable to attend. We know what that means for her. We share her disappointment.

There must be a way. In what we presume to be an absurd effort, we have called the capital. We inquire if some small recognition could be sent to Pat — a card, perhaps.

Two days later. Pat is waiting at the nursing station to go down for treatment. The doors of the elevator open and out steps a handsome, uniformed, debonair, decorated, polished gentleman who steps up to the nursing desk.

"Is Mrs. Pat Rogers here?"

Pat looks up and, in her quick-spoken way, says, "I'm Mrs. Rogers."

He salutes, steps back, and says, "On behalf of the Governor General of Canada, I would like to present you with a token of her acknowledgment. She regrets she cannot personally meet you." He presents her with a signed photograph of the Governor General. He continues to speak with Pat gently and compassionately.

Pat lives to tell the story for weeks to come.

Harvey is in his early fifties. He has leukemia. I know him as a warm guy, a farmer. The solid kind that you read about. The kind who pulls into his neighbor's and harvests the crop and says nothing. It is just what neighbors do. He and his wife have that extra something that comes from facing hardship head-on, together. They have been hoping for a transplant. The news finally came yesterday. No transplant. He is going home to die.

A few minutes ago I stood in my office and said to myself, 'Jevne, get up there. If he has the guts to die, you can at least have the guts to get up there and say good-bye.'

As I enter his room, he is putting on his shirt. His suit jacket is on the bed. It strikes me odd that he wore a suit to the hospital. Quietly, I utter, "I just heard."

Looking me directly in the eye, he points to his suit jacket and says, in a voice that bespeaks his maturity, "It's kind of funny, getting dressed and realizing that in about a week they will be dressing me for my funeral."

We hug. There is an amazing amount of masculine strength in his embrace. I lose the battle to hold back the tears. They seem natural and not inappropriate. There are no words. We say good-bye with no words. Neither of us senses abandonment. This is an unspoken acknowledgment that this is as far as I can walk the walk with him.

The Voice of the Other

A S CHILDREN, WE HAVE AN INNATE SENSE of being at
home in the universe. Of knowing that the world is a place
where we belong. A place that is safe and predictable. A place that
can be trusted. But it isn't long until the sense of alienation begins.
The sense of being "apart from," not really belonging, not being
totally at home.

As adolescents, our alienation is deepened by an awareness
that the world is incongruent with our inner experiences, and by
the conspiracy of silence in which we unconsciously participate. Yet
our hunger persists. We know it as a longing to find home. We
hear the voice of "Other" as a call to a spiritual home. To a place
where our souls belong.

Experience informs us what home is *not*. It is not a place.
Not a single human relationship. Not a trophy case of career
accolades. Not a set of clear-cut answers.

As we move between the dichotomies of life, we feel the pulse

of life, the pull homeward. We feel the tension between giving up and going on. A pulsing logic develops between a sense of being apart and being connected.

Hope happens in the space between. Between the secular and the sacred. Between trust and skepticism. Between the concrete and the intangible. Between evidence and intuition. Between religion and spirituality. Between doubt and faith.

For some, faith comes easily. There is no need to question. No need to be apart from the expected, the traditional. For others, there are just glimpses. Moments when the search seems guided, hopeful. Hoping is noticing that the glimpses are being woven into the fabric of life as a unique tapestry. Creating a pattern that is continually unfolding – sometimes consciously, sometimes outside of our awareness.

Hoping is searching. Searching for a place called home. For a place where doubt and faith co-habit and live in rhythm. Where they cease to compete. Where they mutually inform. We can know the search as a home in itself. Hoping is recognizing that we search, not for a set of premises, but for a relationship, an unnamed relationship that, once embraced fully, leaves no doubt.

The movement between doubt and faith is something that no one talks about. It is as if we are supposed to be able to be believers in a moment. Like Paul on the way to Damascus. No one says, "Faith can grow in you. Until then, you live on hope. You can live on the glimpses. And it is okay to live on the glimpses." No one tells us that life will come in and pound the blazes out of those glimpses. That the challenge is to look for more glimpses. Hoping is saying "yes" to the glimpses. Nobody tells us that life can hurt, even at times when we believe. Hoping is allowing the doubt and the faith. Hoping is accepting that the pulsing between doubt and faith is a natural rhythm.

Hoping is noticing the times when we hear the voice of the "Other." When we experience it as a glimpse. When we sense it as a companion. When we recognize that the Voice calls us home. When we sense that we are being tuned as instruments. When we experience those moments that let us listen to the quiet of our own souls. The moments are like a voice, speaking, asking us to listen. A voice that is not our own and yet we recognize it. We hear it in the unexpected moments. Often in the solitude. In the separateness; not far from the ache. Or in the suffering; not far from the pain. And not only in our own pain, our own suffering. We hear it in the wonder. In the mystery. In the sense of design in the mystery.

Hoping is wanting to go home and not knowing the way. Being willing to listen for directions. And knowing that we are not alone in the search. Sensing "yes," this is the direction. Being able to live with the uncertainty. To take the risks. Feel the pain. Celebrate the moments. Court the glimpses. With the glimpses of the "Other," there is a quiet — a stillpoint in the midst of the seeming chaos, a knowing. A sense of coming home.

Hoping is knowing what is provided is not the musical score but an invitation to the concert. Hoping is coming to know and coming to own the rhythms of our lives along the way. Hoping is knowing we need our weaknesses as much as our strengths. Owning our humanness. Knowing we are connected *and* alone. We are brave *and* afraid. We are just *and* hurtful; helper *and* helped; needy *and* full. Hoping is knowing that the price of going home is not giving up who we are. It is *becoming* who we are.

As a child, I knew the gift of a rainbow. I took joy in every season, saw life in every injured bird, knew quiet in a storm. I loved to ride bareback before dawn and bask in the sweat of helping with the haying. I instinctively knew who and when to trust. I saw a world of abundance and knew it was to be shared. I felt at times one with the universe. God was just *there*. I was home. I could have conversations with that Someone who seemed to know me. My hope was like a tree. I loved trees. Particularly the gnarled ones that seemed to grow right out of rock. That defied the laws of nature for survival. I was intrigued, knowing that what nourishes a tree is only partially visible to the eye.

I have come to an understanding that, just as there is a rhythm to the sea, there is a rhythm to my spirit. Each wave has its separate crest, its own growth and demise. My hope has grown as I noticed that rhythm. For me it became: heart. head. heart. head. ache. search. let go. ache. search. let go. ache. search. let go. quiet. search. quiet. search.

At times it has staccatoed. At times it has created a cacophony. At times, a symphony. Then I have wanted to be able to read the music. I have wanted to know why the composer had chosen each chord. I haven't understood the minor and dissonant chords. I have wanted an explanation for each of the movements. The composer was silent. I wanted to believe in the composer.

I was challenged to accept the statement:

> If all experienced God in the same way and returned Him an identical worship, the song of the church triumphant would have no symphony, it would be like an orchestra in which all the instruments played the same notes.[3]

---

3 C.S. Lewis, *The Problem of Pain*. New York: MacMillan, 1940, p. 138

Eventually the silence has given way to dialogue. The longing, to an intentional search. The drive for certainty, to a celebration of the mystery. Hoping has become the challenge of finding meaning living between the dichotomies. In the place where the rhythm is being worked out. In the place where it is possible to embrace both meaning *and* despair; connectedness *and* separateness; commitment *and* freedom; head *and* heart; faith *and* doubt; life *and* death.

I was only three when my grandpa died. I don't remember, but whenever my mom talks about it, she gets real quiet. She doesn't cry. She just says she misses him "whole bunches." He died in June. She says that on the day he died, it rained and rained and rained. The soft kind of rain that doesn't hurt anything. The kind of rain when my dad says, "We really needed a soaker."

My brother Tommy went over to the window to watch. It was pouring rain so much he couldn't even go out in it. He was real quiet, and after a while he said, "Look, Mom, even God is crying."

Yep, there's a God. Only God could make everything different and everything special. Only frogs have spots, and they aren't *really* ugly. So there has to be a God. I like crickets, too, 'cause of the sounds they make at night. There are tons of them down near the slough. In the summer I get to leave my window open, and even through my curtains I can hear them. My curtains are lined, and they have purple and pink ballerinas on them. I like imagining that they are dancing to the sound of the crickets. I've never been to a real ballet, though. Some people think frogs and crickets and stuff are ugly. Nothin' is really ugly, 'specially frogs. Even if they were, I wouldn't eat their legs! I wouldn't want my leg eaten just 'cause I was ugly.

The trouble with some folks is they think some things are ugly and other things are beautiful. There are some beautiful things that are mean, and some ugly things that are kind. It isn't all that confusing. It looks confusing 'cause people think there's right and wrong, but there really isn't. There is just hurtin' or not hurtin'. If it hurts somebody, you don't do it. If it doesn't hurt anybody, then it's okay. But you have to think of the trees and stuff as somebodies, too — 'cause, after all, they were here before we were. And they hurt, too.

I am sitting on the backless bench in the little chapel at Bible camp. This is probably my last year of camp. I have been here a couple of years as a camper. This year I am a junior counsellor. Bible camp is okay. There are sports all afternoon. We can't swim in the lake, though, or we'll get the itch. I don't really mind, though, because I get ear infections if I go swimming. Every morning a bell tolls at 7:00 a.m.. The sound is really clear. We still have those silly cabin inspections, and probably the baseball captains will all be boys again. They still have the big watermelon party.

It is the first night. The man who is talking in the service isn't like anyone else I ever heard. I don't really like him. He is talking "at" us, telling us we are "a bunch of sinners." I am sitting in silence. I feel like I am being told to stand in the corner for throwing erasers in class and I don't even get to tell my side of the story.

And he is saying everything so loud. It's just a little chapel. He doesn't have to yell. If I was God, I would say, "Stop yelling! I'm not deaf." I wonder how he hears God when he is yelling so loudly.

He's praying now. Sheesh, I am going to get a kink in my neck if he doesn't stop soon. I let my eyes peek around. Everyone else is keeping their eyes closed and their heads down. He is saying, "If you want Jesus in your life, come up here." I am thinking, "If I want Jesus in my life, I am sure He won't mind me staying right here." I can't help but wonder what this guy's going to do when those people get up there. I am fascinated. Some of the group is going up there. Not me. Not on your life. I don't trust that guy. This seems like a circus. Those people look pretty serious, though. It must be right for them. But it sure isn't for me. If I did believe, it seems to me that would be between God and me.

Our church in the country and the town church share the same pastor. I come to the town church every Thursday after school for confirmation classes. This is my second year. I like our church in the country better. I love the way it looks at dusk in the fall, just at harvest. It makes me wonder about the pioneers who chose the spot. I go there alone sometimes and study for exams. I don't feel alone there. Just quiet.

I am a little early today. I like coming early. It's a little church. It only has about eight pews on each side. At the front is a tall picture of Jesus walking on the water. It's really a beautiful painting. The waves look like they are actually moving, and Jesus looks strong and calm. I like just sitting for a few minutes. I don't think. I just sit. I wish we would really talk in confirmation class, but we don't. We have homework, and we go over the homework. And there is lots of memory work that my brother Nels and our friend Chris hardly ever do. I don't know if anyone else feels what I do. It is like a magnet pulling me right from the center of my chest. I feel it more when I am sitting here before class than when we are actually going over lessons.

I have lots of questions. Does anyone else feel that pull? Why is infant baptism so important? Does any one else wonder how a leaf can be so perfect or why so many of the stories are about men? Or if there is something God wants them to do with their lives? Or is it all up to us? And how would we know? And how come we are not supposed to talk about all of these things? Sometimes I ache. I long for the answers.

"Hi, Gram. How are ya?"

"Well hello, Ronna. You haven't been to visit for so long. Where have you been?"

It has only been a week since I last visited, so I'm not sure what to say. She is standing in front of the stove, her starched apron spotless. The smell of pan-fried potatoes is coming from the old iron skillet. She still makes the best home fries. I flounder for something to talk about.

"To Banff. Mom had to go, and so I got to invite a friend to go with us for the whole weekend. Claudette and I went canoeing on the Bow River."

"So. If you were in Banff all weekend, I guess you didn't go to church."

Ah! It feels so good to be able to look at her directly and say, "Oh no, I went to church, Grandma. Claudette is Catholic so she has to. We got up early and went to six o'clock mass."

Her voice changes. Her demeanor condemns. I don't know what I've done.

"You went to a Catholic church? With a Catholic?"

Who does she think I would go to mass with — a Baptist! I feel a wall coming up from my solar plexus and a curtain being drawn between us. The communication has ended. Like it has so many times before. I am learning. For her, there is only one version of religion: *her* version. If I want to live her version, I have to keep up on what's new in sin. This week it is attending mass with a devout Catholic.

I stand in silence before her. What I want to say is, "I can't stay for lunch." The words that come out are, "Is Grandpa home?"

I find him in his shop at the back of the garage. He shuts down the lathe when he sees me. Smiles. Offers me a hard raspberry candy. The kind he keeps everywhere. He offers the piece of wood he has been working on. My fingers test the smoothness. We both smile. He nods his head and restarts the lathe. The shop is really messy, but it feels good just to be there and to watch him.

It's 1:30 a.m.. I ache. I hunger for something. Not something to eat. The hunger is not something physical. I feel like something is missing. I am standing at the window of the lodge looking out at the lake. It's a huge window with crossbars. It is so clear, and the moon is so bright, I can see right across the lake. We are here on a Luther League retreat. Everyone else is asleep. I am trying to listen. I walk back and forth just listening as the moonlight glistens off the water. Listening. I don't even know for what. It is as if I am listening to a part of me deep inside and to Someone outside of myself. It is like they are conversing, and I am only to listen in. There are no words. Yet, there is a sense of communicating. I wonder, 'Is this prayer?' I am aware of the warmth of tears on my face, yet there is no sense of sadness. Just fullness. Puzzling. There is Oneness, too, but I don't really know what I mean by that. And there is an aloneness.

A voice from the far bedroom calls out in a loud whisper: "Ronna?"

"Yes."

"Are you okay?"

"Yes."

"Do you need anything?"

I answer "No" because I don't know how to say, "I want to know what I am feeling. I want to know who I am listening to."

"Okay. Good-night."

I am again with the silence and the aloneness and the questions. And the sense of being spoken to. And I hunger to speak with someone about the Someone I sense.

It was to have been a simple operation. Back at school in a week. Right after New Year's seemed like a good time. But I am sick. Really sick. The actual operation went okay, but I got pneumonia. No one expected a supposedly healthy teenager to get pneumonia. I am trying to print on a pad of paper and nothing is happening. There is no way to say anything.

It was just yesterday, I think, that the nurse who looked like an overweight wrestler in a white uniform folded me into a wheelchair for the journey to X-ray. It was like there was a dagger my right side. It was excruciating. She called me a wimp. Said she saw people who were really hurt in the war. Weeks later they would find and remove two bone chips from the original surgical site, but no one knows that now. I only know the pain. The sheets soaked in ice water are welcome. It's like it's not even my body.

I am in the southwest corner of the ward, away from the windows. Dad is on the left side of the bed, standing; Mom is on the window side, seated and closer to my shoulders. I begin to feel strange. Something odd is happening. I am leaving. I am in the northeast corner, way up, looking down. My body looks peaceful. There is no pain. None. Dad is crying, just tears, no sound. Mom waits. There is no way of explaining what is happening, even to myself. The color in particular is indescribable. Like nothing else I have ever seen: a tangerine mist. I once saw the sunrise strike a valley of fog. That's the closest to the color I've ever seen since.

There is a wall. I don't know any words to describe what I am feeling. There is a Presence. It isn't something or Someone I hear or see. I *feel* a Presence. Somehow I know I am being given a choice. The Presence is speaking to my whole being. The choice is mine: I can leave or I can stay. But this is as far as I can go without deciding. There is no tunnel like I have heard about. It's more like a barrier. The conversation isn't very long. I indicate, "If I go back, it will be so hard." I am somehow aware of Dad's tears. They seem important. The reply is simply, "If you go back, the *Presence* will go with you." The promise seems true.

There is a feeling of quiet as I lie thinking about my dream. It was about an office that I am apparently about to occupy. The office has beautiful coral inlaid marble in the floor and color tones that are stunning, yet gentle. As I walk into it, I sense it has been designed for me, yet I can't make myself, despite obvious intent, go through the doorway. It seems I must first answer a question, audible in the dream only to me: "Are you or are you not going to serve God?" I awoke before I heard my answer.

I run my shower and skip breakfast. I hate breakfast, so missing it is no tragedy. It's late fall. The car is cold and the 8:30 news is on. I am oblivious to both. I am thinking. When I took the job at the hospital, I knew it would be the challenge I had always wanted. It would use all of my knowledge, call on all my skills, and allow for creativity. It was certainly proving to be that. I have good colleagues. For the most part all of us pull together; we somehow know the job is bigger than any of us. As I drive, I can feel my shoulders relax. A gentle smile creeps across my face. At a stop light I can hear myself say, "Look, there is no way we can do this alone. If You've got any help, You better get it down here. I am doing my best, but my best isn't enough. You have to help. I surrender. I give up. I give up knowing what is best or how long it should take or how it will happen. I'll make happen what I can. The big stuff is up to You."

The question, "Is God with me today?" comes to my awareness. I smile as from somewhere the question is flipped to, "Am I with God today?"

"Hello. I am Dr. Jevne. I promised I would come by and see you for a few minutes. I think my colleague Graeme told you about me."

"Oh, yes. I'm so glad you've come. Graeme is so good to me. We can talk about anything."

She is obviously very ill. All I really know about her is that she is in the last days of her life. Just looking at her, I know. Her voice is a near whisper at times. She tells me how it is hard to be in the hospital. How it is necessary but how she misses the neighbors. And most of all her husband. He can't drive any more.

Just as I am about to leave, she clasps my hand and asks, "Will you pray with me?"

Oh, joy! How am I going to get out of this? The squeeze in my hand tells me, 'Not easily!' My pulse accelerates and, with my best psychotherapeutic calm voice, I suggest, "Perhaps we could pray in silence. You could pray your favorite prayer."

Not to be!

She utters, "Oh no, dear. I would much prefer that you pray. I am so weak."

Deep down somewhere in my soul I apologize to God and create the first, and hopefully last, public prayer ever to emit from my mouth. I don't do too badly!

Some days at the bedside, I am not alone. Someone else is present, or Present.

I am going to try again. Maybe there is a place where I can belong, a faith community. When I was growing up, church was going to potluck dinners and knowing someone would be there if you needed help. It was about doing your share. I taught Sunday school. The kids were more interested in coloring Easter eggs than in the Passion story. But that didn't really matter. I was even the pianist for a while, both for church and for choir. They had to limit the music to pieces with no more than four flats. I loved choir. That's what I miss most. We would always go to someone's for coffee after. Just because I was young, I wasn't left out. And it was on a school night! There is still a special place in my heart for so many members of that choir. Freeman, the choirmaster, and his wife, Val, treated me like I was a real adult and a real kid. Freeman played crib with me on Sunday afternoons. It was really hard when he died. With Alec, I had a bet that I wouldn't marry before I was eighteen. Henry sang off key, but that was just Henry. We had a lot of laughs. And we were a good choir, too. It was there that I knew *community*.

Today I am going to try going to a city church for the second time in ten years. I am hungry for that old sense of community. It is worth a second try. I can tell by how many cars there are outside that this is a much bigger church than where I came from. I arrive in plenty of time. Two ushers are standing right inside the door. I take my bulletin and nod my head when one says, "Good morning." I can tell he is more interested in the conversation he is having with the other usher. My eyes search for a seat somewhere where I am not conspicuous. About half way down on the right side will be okay. The music is coming from an organ in the balcony. It is much more sophisticated than what I could play. People are coming in. Many of them know each other. The pews fill up. There are people on all sides of me now, except for my escape route on the right side.

The service begins much like I am accustomed to. There are few surprises until the minister is saying, "Turn to your neighbor and shake hands with them as you greet them with 'Peace be with you.' " The spell is broken. I am no longer here to worship. I am struggling for the protocol. How is this done? I can feel myself hating this. I don't want to say "Peace" to these people. I have no idea who they are. What is this pseudo-intimacy supposed to do? For me, it is like having sex on the first date. It lasts only a moment, but the imprint is everlasting. I can't hear the sermon. The hymns are painful and foreign. I can hardly wait until the service is over. It's long. I have hit the Sunday of the month where they have Communion. I hunger for the sacrament. But I am clear: not here, not now. I feel no awkwardness as I decline the usher's ambivalent invitation.

I am comfortable letting the offering plate pass. I welcome the benediction. It cues the ending of the service. I slip quietly out to the right. An enormously overweight woman has cut off my escape route. I calculate. I confirm there is no way of getting by her. I will have to go up the middle aisle. Fine. Maybe someone will say, "Hello." No one does.

As I drive away, I sense the rationalizing, the voice of reason: "Don't judge on the basis of one effort. Try again next week." At another level, I sense another voice and know. For me, it is not in this church that I will hear the voice of the "Other."

We are different. Norm is big – 6'3" and pushing 200 pounds. I am littler – pushing nearly 105 and proud of my substantiveness. He is theological, philosophical, and bright. I am, at best, a hopeful agnostic, practical, and mediocre in comparison. He is logical. I am intuitive. He has words. I have pictures. He seems complex. I feel simple. He has thoughts. I have feelings. He has passion for life. I am weary of challenge. He thrashes. I flow. We both can laugh.

I want his knowing of God. He wants my trust in the "universe." My metaphorical language annoys him. His philosophical language is foreign to me. Each of us thinks the other is withholding evidence. At times he is an intellectual irritant to me. At other times, a willing mentor. Sometimes, though, interacting with him feels like carrying on a conversation with a polar bear in a pup tent.

Like on our four-hour drive to the conference.

The prairie, the parkland, and the foothills slip by unnoticed as his verbal barrage goes on. He is a formidable sparring partner. The rules are simple: No mercy, no prisoners! Both trained in the same philosophy department, we have similar tools for discourse, but I am no match for his relentless demand that I be accountable for my views. For his insistence that I be known. I eventually speak the pain rather than the logic of my wrestlings:

"I find it difficult to *believe* in God, not to *experience* God. Believing and experiencing are different. I have difficulty believing, not because of the unfairness of wars or the unexplainable suffering I see, but because, at times, I lose touch with my experience of God. I lose it more often in a medical records meeting than at the bedside.

"I wish I could say, 'Here! Here! Here! Here are my beliefs about God.' I cannot. I can say, 'Here is my experience of nature. Here is my experience of dying people. Here is my experience of the strength of the human spirit. Here is my experience of despair.' "

We drive on in silence for some time. But not in aloneness.

The letter from Norm is complicated, caring and direct. For a "polar bear," rather gentle. I read and reread and reread one paragraph. Like some of our conversations, it requires unpacking:

> Our citizenship is in another country, and we travel in a foreign land. It is a land we can love and sometimes feel comfortable in, but in which we cannot quite feel at home ... We are touched in the deepest part as God reaches through the mist, and past reason, and gently touches us at the heart of all that matters. Such a touch unalterably alters the vision. In a sense we may not see more, we certainly see differently. Once touched, that place in our lives is forever a point of departure ... It is always a course of yielding or refusing, of walking or stalking.

I feel a sense of being understood. As if someone has broken the silence. Someone else has spoken directly of the yearning, of the fullness. I know someone else knows the sense of hungering for home. A hungering that I can no longer set aside. A hunger not satisfied with the deep-felt bond of a good marriage, the challenges of a demanding career, or the accolades of achievement. But where is home?

That night a dream informs but doesn't explain:

> I am in a chamber of crystals. No one else is here. It is very lonely in the chamber. Very few people come here. There is no map. I seem to get here by letting go. I stand quietly in the midst of the beauty. It is the magnificence of the crystals that suggests more than an accidental geographical fault, but I cannot know. I can only sense. I can only sense the totalness of the beauty. The treasures are so plentiful and the crystals so plentiful, there is no need to even think of hoarding. One simply takes what is needed. This is a place so beautiful, all ugliness is an illusion. A place so bountiful, scarcity is a myth. A place so accessible, all anxiety is unnecessary.

There is a sense that this is somehow home.

I have awakened feeling literally in the midst of what I suspect is prayer. There seems to be a pattern developing. There's an initial sense of quiet, a deep sense of gratitude for a new day, a reflection about whom I want cared for during the day, and a request: "Simply let me be quiet with whatever happens today. May I simply do that which can be done. And may I do it with kindness."

The quiet is a good feeling. It comes back at times during the day. I seem to be able to notice it in my voice. It's a tone that is qualitatively different. It has a similarity to the voice I hear in the mornings. The voice that is there when I am listening. The voice that this morning said, "Practice."

"Practice what?"

"Each day. Just practice. Let go."

"Of what?"

"Of trying."

"Are you really there?"

"Do we need to go over that again? Sense. Am I present? Can you deny me? Deny me? See how you feel."

"I cannot deny you. I just don't know what to do with you."

"That will unfold. Right now, just practice. Grow in love and strength. All else will unfold."

I feel like the slow kid in class. Like in high school when I never caught on to combinations and permutations — no matter who explained them.

In the classroom of life, I wonder if God has a "turtle" row.

Driving along the ocean toward the airport, I feel a sense of quiet despite the intensity of these last few days spent observing at a pain clinic and bone marrow transplant unit. I am feeling grateful for my health. My commitment to life has deepened.

As I cross the bridge, it is partially obscured in the ocean fog. Fog has always fascinated me. When it is thick, the rest of the world is nonexistent. I like knowing something is there when I cannot see it. I sense faith is like that: believing something is out there. Sensing you have navigated the territory before. Knowing where the danger is. Going blindly into the fog. With confidence.

With hope, it is different. Hope offers no assurances. There are only glimpses. To know, we must cross the bridge, not knowing yet trusting. Without crossing, we can never know. We can go slowly, but we can never know without going forward. To move toward the assurance, we must face the fear. So it is with me. I am not blessed with the sense of assurance that satisfies the academic mind. I have unanswered questions. I bask in the mystery and yet hunger for the assurance. I am crossing the bridge of hope.

Tears begin to stream down my face. No sobbing. No language or thought to accompany them. No sense of a "psychological" distress. This is not a dominantly emotional experience. It passes.

At the airport I return the car and board the plane with only a few words and nods of the head. The flight is uneventful. It feels good to get home. I am glad no one is at home. I can have a few minutes to myself.

As I turn on the shower, I am aware of a powerful anger — virtually a rage, yet with no visible sign of emotion. 'What is this about?' I am more fascinated than concerned about my response. The words that go with what I am sensing are, 'I am alone.' In that instant the rage transforms to sadness and then strangely to peace. Then, a powerful sense of, 'I am *not* alone.'

I am left quiet and strong. I am left with a sense of where home is.

Epilogue

ONLY WEEKS AGO Allen and I sat in a noisy White Spot in Vancouver enjoying watching Norm kid the waitress. He had a way of affirming people with his humor. The discussion turned intentionally to hope. I specifically wanted Norm's feedback on a understanding of hope that was emerging from our research.

I launched into a description mapped out on a napkin. "What do you think? You're the best analytical mind I know, so give me the straight goods. But, remember, I cry easy."

The pause was lengthy. The questions few. I waited for him to point out the philosophical error I may have made. Instead, his voice quieted. The smile was gentle. The eyes direct, yet awkward. The words sincere. "When you folks started talking about hope a couple of years ago, I thought you were out to lunch. The idea of creating a center for the understanding of hope escaped me." A snicker reminded all of us of the many debates over the years. An earnestness returned to his tone. His exact words have faded, but the message stays clear. He sincerely believed in what we are doing.

His last sentence is etched in my memory: "In all of this, there is the hand of God."

That was only weeks ago.

- - - - - -

I cannot escape the sense of molten lava having hardened in my chest. Tonight I have driven over to the house where The Hope Foundation will open within a couple of months. A good friend has come with me. She knew me as a kid. She had the impossible challenge of teaching me singing. We have been friends for thirty years. She was the one I called last September when they said I had a major reoccurrence. I called her, not to fuss or to share my fear, but to make sure someone would hold me to the lifestyle changes that I had become negligent about.

As we walk about the four stories of the Hope House, she asks, "Why did you want to show me the House tonight? I know you well enough to know that things are not always as they seem."

I am hesitant to speak. I don't really know what to say. "All I know is that I needed to come to a house of hope tonight. I needed to remind myself that we know so little. That things may not even be ours to know. That the questions that must be asked in this building must be about the ground and nature of hope, not solely about the outcomes of hope. I needed to come here to be intentional about hope. To remind myself of what there is to be grateful for. To remind myself that being impotent is not grounds for despair. To be intentional about finding a rightful place for the despair."

I paused, then added, "Norm, who pointed to that rightful place, to that sense of where home is, has just been diagnosed with advanced inoperable cancer. I needed to come here to feel his presence. To embrace his strength."

I didn't tell her that coming to the House was a way of praying. A prayer of commitment to live life fully – pain and all – from a place I name hope.

Norman Roderick Coppin, Ph.D., died July 8, 1993.

Hope House, under the auspices of The Hope Foundation of Alberta, officially opened October 5, 1993.

To live with hope is
To live a prayer
Of gratitude.
For all of life.

Not for this or for that
But for life.
All of life.
For the pain.
  The laughter.
  The deep.
  The shallow.
  The clear.
  The obscure.
For the sane
  and the absurd.
For the hurt.
For the healing.
For the ugly and the beautiful.
Even for the hatred.

Most of all
For the love.

About the Hope House

At Hope House our mission is to learn about hope. To understand how people live through difficult circumstances. To learn how each person, in unique ways, uses hope. Of particular interest is what strengthens hope and what injures or destroys hope. The way we learn is by sharing with each other. As we learn, we also share with others what we have learned through workshops, counselling, and community projects.

Hope House is sponsored by The Hope Foundation of Alberta, a registered nonprofit organization dedicated to understanding and enhancing hope in individuals, families, and institutions. The Foundation has three arms: hope through helping, hope through understanding, and hope through the arts. The Foundation is a joint community/university venture where people from all walks of life cooperate in practical and scholarly activities, coordinated at the Hope House located on campus.

If you have something to share with us or for further information contact:

The Hope Foundation of Alberta
c/o Dr. R. Jevne
Department of Educational Psychology
6-102 Education North
Faculty of Education
University of Alberta
Edmonton, Alberta
Canada T6G 2G5

About the Author

Ronna Fay Jevne, a psychologist and professor, began her career as a teacher and school counsellor. A personal illness and years of working with cancer patients are the genesis of her passion to understand hope.

Dr. Jevne holds graduate degrees in Educational Philosophy, Theological Studies, and Counselling Psychology. She teaches in the graduate division of Counselling Psychology in the Department of Educational Psychology at the University of Alberta, Edmonton, Canada. Her dream of a center to study and enhance hope is now a reality. "Hope House" extends her work beyond her original work with cancer patients to those who suffer various forms of adversity.

Her interdisciplinary perspective on "hope work" is enjoyed locally, nationally, and internationally by audiences of health care providers, psychologists, educators, clergy, and the general public.

Dr. Jevne's husband, Allen, shares her work and passion for hope. Together they also share three children, three foster children, and three grandchildren.

Her love of photography, as evidenced by the photographs in this book, is her special way of embracing the creative and of returning to her *self* through solitude.

Other LuraMedia Publications

BANKSON, MARJORY ZOET

Braided Streams:
Esther and a Woman's Way of Growing

Seasons of Friendship:
Naomi and Ruth as a Pattern

"This Is My Body. . .":
Creativity, Clay, and Change

BORTON, JOAN

Drawing from the Women's Well: *Reflections on the Life Passage of Menopause*

CARTLEDGE-HAYES, MARY

To Love Delilah:
Claiming the Women of the Bible

DARIAN, SHEA

Seven Times the Sun:
Guiding Your Child through the Rhythms of the Day

DOHERTY, DOROTHY ALBRACHT
and McNAMARA, MARY COLGAN

Out of the Skin Into the Soul:
The Art of Aging

DUERK, JUDITH

Circle of Stones:
Woman's Journey to Herself

I Sit Listening to the Wind:
Woman's Encounter within Herself

GOODSON, WILLIAM (with Dale J.)

Re-Souled: *Spiritual Awakenings of a Psychiatrist and his Patient in Alcohol Recovery*

JEVNE, RONNA FAY

It All Begins With Hope:
Patients, Caretakers, and the Bereaved Speak Out

The Voice of Hope:
Heard Across the Heart of Life

with ALEXANDER LEVITAN
No Time for Nonsense:
Getting Well Against the Odds

KEIFFER, ANN

Gift of the Dark Angel: *A Woman's Journey through Depression toward Wholeness*

LAIR, CYNTHIA

Feeding the Whole Family: *Down-to-Earth Cookbook and Whole Foods Guide*

LODER, TED

Eavesdropping on the Echoes:
Voices from the Old Testament

Guerrillas of Grace:
Prayers for the Battle

Tracks in the Straw:
Tales Spun from the Manger

Wrestling the Light:
Ache and Awe in the Human-Divine Struggle

MEYER, RICHARD C.

One Anothering: *Biblical Building Blocks for Small Groups*

NELSON, G. LYNN

Writing & Being: *Taking Back Our Lives through the Power of Language*

O'HALLORAN, SUSAN and DELATTRE, SUSAN

The Woman Who Lost Her Heart:
A Tale of Reawakening

PRICE, H.H.

Blackberry Season:
A Time to Mourn, A Time to Heal

RAFFA, JEAN BENEDICT

The Bridge to Wholeness:
A Feminine Alternative to the Hero Myth

Dream Theatres of the Soul:
Empowering the Feminine through Jungian Dreamwork

ROTHLUEBBER, FRANCIS

Nobody Owns Me: *A Celibate Woman Discovers her Sexual Power*

RUPP, JOYCE

The Star in My Heart:
Experiencing Sophia, Inner Wisdom

SAURO, JOAN

Whole Earth Meditation:
Ecology for the Spirit

SCHNEIDER-AKER, KATHERINE

God's Forgotten Daughter:
A Modern Midrash: What If Jesus Had Been A Woman?

WEEMS, RENITA J.

I Asked for Intimacy: *Stories of Blessings, Betrayals, and Birthings*

Just a Sister Away: *A Womanist Vision of Women's Relationships in the Bible*

LuraMedia, Inc.
7060 Miramar Rd., Suite 104
San Diego, CA 92121

Books for Healing and Hope,
Balance and Justice
Call 1-800-FOR-LURA for information.